First published in 2007 by New Holland Publishers (UK) Ltd
London • Cape Town • Sydney • Auckland
Garfield House, 86–88 Edgware Road, London W2 2EA, United Kingdom
www.newhollandpublishers.com
80 McKenzie Street, Cape Town 8001, South Africa
14 Aquatic Drive, Frenchs Forest, NSW 2086, Australia
218 Lake Road, Northcote, Auckland
ISBN 978 1 84537 483 9
10 9 8 7 6 5 4 3 2 1
Editorial Direction: Rosemary Wilkinson Editor: Anne Konopelski Production: Hazel Kirkman
Designed and created for New Holland by AG&G Books Copyright © 2004 "Specialist" AG&G Books
Design: Glyn Bridgewater Illustrations: Dawn Brend, Gill Bridgewater and Coral Mula
Editor: Alison Copland Photographs: see page 80
Reproduction by Pica Digital Pte Ltd, Singapore
Printed and bound in Malaysia by Times Offset (M) Sdn. Bhd.
The information in this book is true and complete to the best of our knowledge. All recommendations
are made without guarantee on the part of the authors and the publishers. The authors and publishers
disclaim any liability for damages or injury resulting from the use of this information.

The
BAMBOO, GRASS & PALM
Specialist

The essential guide to selecting, growing and propagating bamboos, grasses and palms

David Squire
Series editors: A. & G. Bridgewater

Contents

Author's foreword

Bamboos, grasses and palms have such a wide range of leaf and stem shapes and sizes that they can be used to create many types of garden, from the exotic to cottage-style. These plants vary widely in size, from tufted and low grasses to bamboos 6 m (20 ft) or more high. Their roles in gardens are diverse, and range from forming screens to stabilizing banks; they can also be grown as specimen plants in lawns, or in containers on patios. Few gardeners can resist the relaxing effect of a bamboo 'walk' (see page 11).

Many gardeners hesitate to plant bamboos, believing all of them to be invasive and to cause damage to ponds and patios, as well as intruding into neighbouring gardens. Some bamboos are rampant, but

many are clump-forming and will not cause any damage. There are also mechanical ways to prevent and reduce their spread.

The beauty of bamboos is to be found not only in their sizes, but also in their vibrant leaves and canes – the picture-parades of bamboos within this colourful book will enable you to select the right species to bring that extra bit of colour to your garden and patio.

A few carefully chosen bamboos, ornamental grasses or palms will help you create a distinctive yet easily managed garden. This practical yet inspirational book reveals many exciting ways to use and look after these fascinating plants.

Measurements

Both metric and imperial measurements are given in this book – for example, 1.8 m (6 ft).

NAME CHANGES

Each year, botanists alter the names of some plants, and in recent years bamboos in particular have incurred radical changes. Therefore, in addition to up-to-date botanical names, earlier ones are included in this book. This will enable you to recognize their names from earlier books and plant catalogues, as well as ensuring that you buy the right plants.

SEASONS

Throughout this book, advice is given about seasonal tasks. Because of global and even regional variations in climate and temperature, the four main seasons have been used, with each subdivided into 'early', 'mid-' and 'late' – for example, early spring, mid-spring and late spring. These 12 divisions of the year can be applied to the appropriate calendar months in your local area if you find this helps.

What are bamboos, grasses and palms?

Bamboos, ornamental grasses and palms have varied habits. All bamboos are evergreen and have a semi-woody nature, while ornamental grasses are herbaceous, hardy or half-hardy annuals, or perennials. Palms are evergreen and only a few of these mainly tropical and subtropical plants are sufficiently hardy for planting outdoors in temperate regions. Many are ideal for growing indoors.

What are their growth habits?

TALKING BOTANICALLY

Bamboos

Bamboos usually have two different types of root system; either clump-forming or running.

→ Clump-forming rhizomes
Pachymorphic root systems create dense clumps of rhizomes, freely branching and usually with short spaces between their joints. Buds forming on the rhizome produce fresh culms (canes).

↓ Running rhizomes
Leptomorphic root systems are spreading in nature, with long and running rhizomes that have both culm (cane) buds as well as others that enable the rhizome to grow and spread. Such root systems are invasive.

MAKING THE RIGHT CHOICE

Choosing non-invasive bamboos is important in many gardens and the invasive nature of these magnificent plants is described on pages 24–25.

Ornamental grasses

Some are raised annually from seed and others are herbaceous, creating a display for many years. Those that are perennial and evergreen, such as *Cortaderia selloana* (Pampas Grass) create distinctive silvery and silky plumes of flowers that are especially attractive when covered with frost.

What are sedges?
Sedges belong to the Cyperaceae family. They differ from grasses in having stems, often triangular, with solid cross-sections. The stems of grasses are round and hollow. Sedges have a rhizomatous rooting system, with some developing a clump-forming nature and others forming roots that spread. Some are deciduous, others evergreen, and in general sedges need more moisture in the soil than grasses.

What are rushes?
Rushes belong to the Juncaceae, a small family that thrives in sunny, open marsh land, and they are ideal for planting alongside streams and pools. They are perennial, with creeping, rhizomatous roots; in cross-section their stems are round, with leaves at their bases either cylindrical or flat.

PALMS

CANE PALMS

These are distinctive palms, with tall, reed like stems that when mature resemble those of bamboos (see pages 76–77).

FEATHER PALMS

They have fronds (leaves) that are divided on both sides of the midrib. There are many palms with this nature (see pages 76–77).

FISHTAIL PALMS

There are only a few palms with this nature; the ends of the leaflets are wedge-shaped and resemble fish tails (see pages 76–77).

FAN PALMS

These have fan like fronds, attractively split into many segments, partly or wholly divided from one another (see pages 76–77).

Using bamboos in gardens

Bamboos can be used in many ways in gardens and often in borders, side by side with shrubs and other plants. They can form attractive screens and hedges, as well as creating ground cover on banks and alongside rustic paths. Many are ideal for planting in containers on a patio or terrace and are essential parts of Japanese gardens, either planted in the soil or in containers. Before planting a bamboo, check that it will not become invasive (see page 25).

LOW CONTAINER DISPLAY

Pleioblastus viridistriatus is ideal for planting in a container. For other bamboos that are suitable for growing in containers, see pages 12–13.

COLOURFUL CANES

Many bamboos have attractive, colourful canes, and a wide range of these plants is featured on page 22.

FEATURE BAMBOOS

BAMBOOS AS SCREENS

Several bamboos can help to create dramatic and dense screens (see pages 18–19 for planting suggestions and other tips).

BAMBOOS AS WINDBREAKS

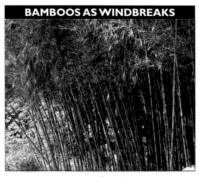

Bamboos used as windbreaks create a congenial and sheltered environment for other plants (see pages 18–19).

Some bamboos, such as Chusquea culeou, are unusual and can be used to create distinctive features (see page 16).

TALL CONTAINER DISPLAY

Tall bamboos, such as Pseudosasa japonica, *create dominant displays in containers (see pages 12–13).*

COLOURFUL LEAVES

Many bamboos, including Sasaella masamuneana 'Albostriata', *have attractive leaves (see page 23 for others).*

DRAMATIC BORDER FEATURES

Many bamboos, including Phyllostachys aureosulcata aureocaulis, *create distinctive features in borders. Related species are featured on pages 41–44.*

SCREEN

Phyllostachys aurea, *together with its many forms (see page 41), creates a lax and open screen that is perfect for an informal garden. For other screening choices, see pages 18–19.*

HEALING SOUNDS AND TEXTURES

As well as being famed for their visual beauty, bamboos have a reputation for being healing and calming, thanks to the rustling of their leaves and their smooth and tactile surfaces.

- **Blowing in the wind:** Bamboos create gentle, rustling sounds when blown by light wind; they introduce a comforting quality to the garden through their repetitious but uneven notes. Tall bamboos alongside gravel paths (which also produce a distinctive noise when trodden on) is one source of sound, while for a surrounding and ultimately enclosing sound theatre consider a bamboo 'walk' (see page 11), where bamboos are planted on both sides of a path and will eventually arch across it.
- **The healing touch:** Most bamboos have smooth, long and narrow leaves that can be gently stroked and run through your fingers. This empathic action, which can help you get to know plants, generates solace and comfort, perhaps in the same way in which stroking a dog or cat is credited with reducing blood pressure and lowering the pulse rate.
- **Medicinal values:** Some bamboos, including *Phyllostachys nigra* (Black-stemmed Bamboo), have healing qualities. The roots were used in Chinese medicine to treat kidney problems, while the fresh canes, when heated, exude sap that has been used in the same way as aspirin.

Using ornamental grasses in gardens

How can I use them?

Ornamental grasses are used in many ways and, increasingly, borders and beds are totally dedicated to herbaceous types. Annual grasses can be used to fill gaps in mixed and herbaceous borders, while tufted or arching types are planted in containers on patios and terraces. The perennial and evergreen Pampas Grass is dramatic and ideal as a focal point in a circular bed in a large lawn. Its plume-like flowerheads are especially attractive when coated in snow.

ORNAMENTAL GRASSES

ANNUAL GRASSES

Some grasses are annuals; others are perennials but usually grown as annuals. It is best to divide Pennisetum setaceum *'Rubrum' (Tender Purple Fountain Grass) because it does not always produce seed.*

PERENNIAL GRASSES

Perennial grasses create colourful and distinctive borders for many years. The clump-forming Miscanthus sinensis *(Japanese Silver Grass) can be planted in borders of herbaceous plants and shrubs.*

DRAMATIC FLOWERHEADS

The hardy annual Hordeum jubatum *(Squirrel-tail Grass) has very distinctive flowerheads that can be dried and dyed for use in indoor floral displays. In borders, it is sown where it will grow.*

LEAF AND FLOWER COLOUR

As well as having attractive leaves, many cultivars of the perennial Miscanthus sinensis *(Japanese Silver Grass) have colourful flowerheads. Shown above is the popular cultivar 'Rotsilber'.*

DOMINANT DISPLAYS

The herbaceous perennial Miscanthus oligostachyus, *although smaller than the more widely grown* Miscanthus sinensis *(Japanese Silver Grass), creates dramatic features in borders, and it is low-growing enough to be planted along a border's edge.*

EVERGREEN GRASS

Few grasses are as dramatic as Cortaderia selloana *(Pampas Grass), with its silky flower plumes. The species grows up to 2.7 m (9 ft) high, but the cultivar 'Pumila' (shown here) is slightly smaller and is ideal for planting as a feature in a lawn in a small garden.*

GRASSES FOR SCREENING

Calamagrostis x acutiflora *'Karl Foerster' (Feather Reedgrass) is a rhizomatous-rooted perennial, eventually growing to about 1.8 m (6 ft) high, which is ideal for forming an unusual and attractive summer screen.*

GRASSES IN CONTAINERS

The cascading nature of Hakonechloa macra *'Alboaurea' makes it ideal for planting either in a container on a patio or at the edge of a raised bed.*

MIXING AND MATCHING GRASSES

Many grasses can be encouraged to create better displays if you plant them in association with other plants. Some of these include:

- *Miscanthus sinensis* **'Zebrinus'** (Zebra Grass; see page 68) is superb when planted with a frill of *Bergenia cordifolia*, which has large, glossy, mid-green, leathery, rounded leaves and bell-shaped, lilac-rose flowers borne in drooping heads.
- *Phalaris arundinacea* **var.** *picta* (Gardeners' Garters; see page 70) has foliage that is perfectly highlighted by *Papaver orientale* (Oriental Poppy) and *Santolina chamaecyparissus*, with their silvery, woolly leaves and bright lemon-yellow flowers that are borne in mid-summer.
- *Stipa pennata* (Feather Grass; see page 71) makes a good companion for *Eschscholzia californica* (Californian Poppy), a hardy annual with finely cut, blue-green leaves and masses of bright orange-yellow flowers throughout most of summer and into autumn. Alternatively, use *Papaver rhoeas* (Field Poppy); it produces spectacular red flowers with black centres during summer.

Sedges and rushes

These are distinctive, moisture-loving plants (see page 3). The popular rush *Juncus effusus spiralis* (Corkscrew Rush) is ideal for planting in a pond with water up to 7.5 cm (3 in) deep. The sedge *Carex oshimensis* 'Evergold' (also known as *Carex morrowii* 'Evergold') is superb for planting in moisture-retentive soil, as well as in a container (see page 58).

Carex oshimensis 'Evergold'

Using palms in gardens

How can I use palms outdoors?

Most palms are tropical or subtropical in origin. Therefore, in temperate climates there are only a few that are reliable outdoors, and even then only in mild areas. Nevertheless, they are dramatic plants and introduce a Mediterranean aura to gardens. They can be used in borders with other plants, or as features in a lawn. Some palms, such as *Trachycarpus fortunei* (Windmill Palm), have attractive trunks covered in coarse, black fibres.

OUTDOORS (TEMPERATE REGIONS)

TALL AND DRAMATIC

LOW AND DRAMATIC

Above: Chamaerops humilis *(Dwarf Fan Palm) usually forms a dense cluster of greyish-green, fan-shaped leaves. However, some forms develop distinctive trunks.*

Left: Trachycarpus fortunei *(Windmill Palm) creates large, fan-shaped leaves formed of narrow, folded segments on stalks that grow up to 90 cm (3 ft) long.*

Using palms and cycads indoors

Many palms are suitable for growing indoors in pots and other containers, including varieties with cane-like stems and those with fan-, feather- and fishtail-like leaves. Some are small enough, especially when they are young, to be displayed on side tables, whereas others are large and dominant and ideal for positioning on the floor and perhaps in a corner. A few cycads, such as the slow-growing *Cycas revoluta* (Sago Palm), can be grown indoors.

How can I use palms indoors?

INDOORS AND IN CONSERVATORIES (TEMPERATE REGIONS)

FOSSIL-LIKE FEATURE

Although eventually growing to more than 1.8 m (6 ft) high in its native Japan, as a houseplant Cycas revoluta *(Sago Palm) is slow-growing and usually less than 60 cm (2 ft) high. Often, it develops only one new leaf each year.*

FEATHER-LIKE FRONDS

Phoenix roebelenii *(Miniature Date Palm) produces feather-like fronds. When young it is ideal for growing indoors, but later needs a conservatory.*

FISHTAIL APPEARANCE

Caryota mitis *(Fishtail Palm) has very distinctive, wedge-shaped leaflets. In India and Southeast Asia, it grows to more than 4.5 m (15 ft) high outdoors, but the height will be much less when grown indoors.*

Bamboos for all gardens

Are bamboos suitable for borders?

Bamboos are versatile plants, and can either be planted in borders that are totally dedicated to them or mixed with shrubs and herbaceous perennials. Bamboos generally have to be mixed with other plants in small gardens, but this need not be a problem because many bamboos have a compact but attractive habit and are ideal for growing in small areas (see pages 25–27 for a wide range of clump-forming and non-invasive bamboos).

BORDER WITH A MEDLEY OF PLANTS WITH DIFFERENT GROWTH HABITS

In most gardens, a mixture of shrubs and clumps of bamboos, with smaller plants such as ferns, ornamental grasses and sedges (see pages 56–71) and herbaceous perennials, creates an attractive medley. However, herbaceous perennials with brightly coloured flowers never harmonize as well with bamboos as do those with attractive leaves, such as *Pulmonaria, Hosta, Houttuynia, Rheum* and *Rodgersia,* and a ground carpeting of ivies, *Tiarella,*

polygonums and *Tolmiea menziesii* (Pig-a-back Plant), which is an ideal ground-covering plant. The mystical *Mandragora officinarum* (European Mandrake) blends well with bamboos and has roots that are said to increase sexual desire and fertility. People once claimed that the branched roots screamed when pulled from the earth. In general, plants that prefer woodland conditions are those that best suit bamboos, and they have the bonus of creating an informal feature.

BAMBOOS AND OTHER BORDER PLANTS

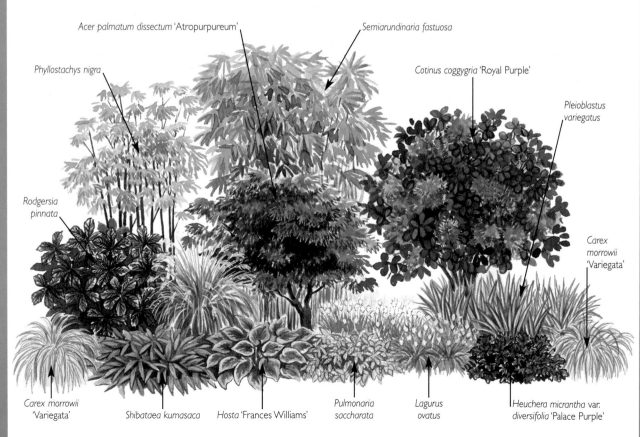

Acer palmatum dissectum 'Atropurpureum'

Semiarundinaria fastuosa

Phyllostachys nigra

Cotinus coggygria 'Royal Purple'

Pleioblastus variegatus

Rodgersia pinnata

Carex morrowii 'Variegata'

Carex morrowii 'Variegata'

Shibataea kumasaca

Hosta 'Frances Williams'

Pulmonaria saccharata

Lagurus ovatus

Heuchera micrantha var. *diversifolia* 'Palace Purple'

Mixing bamboos with other plants enriches a border and each year helps to extend the period of colour and interest. Variegated bamboos, as well as other plants, provide further colour.

Bamboo 'walks'

Pseudosasa japonica

There is a relaxed and rustic quality about a wide gravel path with tall bamboos planted on both sides and canes that partly splay over the path, revealing a narrow strip of sky. A mixture of bamboos is better than one species; alternate tall species with medium-height ones (see pages 26–27 for a range of heights).

If gaps between canes at eye height enable you to see other parts of the garden – and added seclusion and privacy are desired – erect a 1.8 m (6 ft) high screen of bamboo panelling as a background. This screen need not be as substantial and strong as a fence, but will form an attractive background.

DO BAMBOOS FLOWER?

The idea that bamboos flower once every hundred years and then die is a myth that needs to be dispelled.

- Records indicate that flowering within a species is irregular. For example, *Phyllostachys aurea* has been known to flower at 28-, 18- and 14-year intervals.
- Some people claim, incorrectly, that within a species flowering occurs throughout the world at the same time, followed by death. However, it is true that clumps of the same species within a garden sometimes flower at the same time, but this may be because they have all been raised from the same stock.
- The claim that a clump of bamboo invariably dies after flowering is another myth. Sometimes only a few canes within a clump will flower, and the clump soon recovers. Flowering causes a radical depletion of the plant's resources, however, and often complete clumps die, especially if flowering continues over a long period.
- Recovery from flowering is possible, especially if only a few canes have flowered, but when the entire plant flowers it will appear scruffy. You can encourage recovery by regular feeding and watering, although some gardeners prefer to dig up the 'miscreant' bamboo, especially if it is in a small garden.

UPS AND DOWNS OF FLOWERING

Earlier in India – when a single species sometimes covered a large area – the economic loss of cane development was often compensated by an abundance of seed, which could be eaten like rice. However, in Brazil the flowering of indigenous bamboos in the 1800s is claimed to have produced such an abundance of seed that it twice caused plagues of mice and rats.

BORDER DEDICATED SOLELY TO BAMBOOS

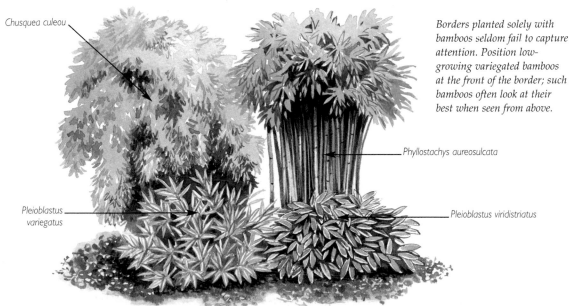

Chusquea culeou

Pleioblastus variegatus

Phyllostachys aureosulcata

Pleioblastus viridistriatus

Borders planted solely with bamboos seldom fail to capture attention. Position low-growing variegated bamboos at the front of the border; such bamboos often look at their best when seen from above.

Bamboos in containers

Many bamboos grow remarkably well in containers displayed on a patio or terrace. The range of bamboos for containers is wide and, while some are relatively low, others are tall and dominant (see opposite page). Especially avoid putting tall ones in windswept positions. Some bamboos have attractively variegated leaves, while others are totally green, but nevertheless attractive. Contrast variegated forms by interspersing them with all-green types.

Are bamboos suitable for containers?

CHOOSING CONTAINERS

Ornate containers are superb for use in Japanese-style gardens

Traditional barrel-type containers are ideal for rustic gardens

Square containers, with fancy decorations, have a clinical nature

Plain, square, wooden containers are ideal for relaxed, informal patios

Fargesia dracocephala, with its shiny, mid-green leaves, creates a tall and dominant feature in a container.

Large pots, wooden tubs or square boxes are ideal homes for bamboos (see below for sizes). Ornate, wide-based pots are ideal for low-growing bamboos, especially when they are positioned in exotic gardens. Large tubs and square boxes are better suited for taller-growing bamboos, and are usually left in one position until the compost is congested with canes and division is necessary.

COMPOST FOR POTS AND CONTAINERS

It is possible to fill a container with garden soil, but this may introduce pests that highlight the vagaries of ordinary garden soil. It is far better to use a mixture of equal parts peat-based compost and loam-based potting compost; the peat-based type increases the compost's ability to retain moisture, while the loam-based type introduces fertilizers and gives containers greater stability, which is essential in windy areas near to the corners of buildings.

For small, low-growing bamboos a container holding at least 10 litres of compost – the equivalent of about 2.5 gallons – is essential. Tubs and square boxes, which suit tall bamboos, need to be large enough to hold 30 litres or more of compost. This is equal to about 8 gallons.

Small pots are usually portable, and bamboos can be planted before you position the container. However, tubs or square boxes are best filled and planted *in situ*. When doing this, ensure that the best and most attractive side of the plant faces towards the main viewing position.

Pleioblastus variegatus, with its pale green leaves streaked in white, creates a low display and is ideal for placing on a patio in a small garden.

PLANTING BAMBOOS IN CONTAINERS

Ensure that the container is clean and suits the area – it should be decorative for exotic areas but rustic for more rural settings.

Step 3
Carefully draw and firm compost in layers around the roots until the surface is about 2.5 cm (1 in) below the container's rim. This will allow for later settlement of the compost, and after a month or so it will leave a watering depth of about 36 mm (1½ in).

Step 2
Fill the container to about half full with compost (see page 12 for the mixture). Gently firm it. Place the bamboo on top and check that the surface of the soil ball is about 36 mm (1½ in) below the rim.

Step 4
Use a watering-can – with the rose turned upwards – to water the compost. Several waterings will be necessary before the compost is thoroughly moist.

Step 1
Check that drainage holes in the base are not blocked. Place a large tub in position; small ones can be moved later. Stand large wooden tubs on three bricks to reduce the risk of the base remaining wet and decaying. Fill the base with broken pieces of clay pots or a thin layer of pebbles.

Take care ...

- Use clean, moisture-retentive compost, not garden soil.

- Stand the container out of direct sunlight.

- Position the container out of strong draughts that dry the compost and foliage.

- Use large containers, especially for tall bamboos. Large containers hold more compost than small ones and are less likely to dry out rapidly in summer.

- Keep the compost moist – it may mean watering several times a day during summer.

Winter care ...

- During winter – especially in cold and exposed areas – the relatively small amount of compost in containers is in danger of freezing and damaging the roots of bamboos. Therefore, in autumn reduce the amount of water added to the compost, keeping it slightly moist rather than saturated.

- If winters are especially severe, wrap the container and compost in straw and sacking. Also closely cloak the sacking and straw in a sheet of polythene to prevent them becoming wet and subsequently freezing. Remove these coverings as soon as the weather improves.

- Bamboos in small containers are especially at risk during winter and can be placed in a cold greenhouse.

- If the canes and leaves become covered with snow, gently shake them before it freezes. Lightly tapping the foliage with a long cane is another way of removing unfrozen snow.

Congested plants

When the compost is congested with roots, in mid-spring either repot the plant into a larger container or remove, divide and repot the divisions in 2–3 pots. Always thoroughly water the compost and keep it moist in summer, especially during the first two years.

BAMBOOS FOR CONTAINERS

Low displays in containers
* *Pleioblastus pygmaeus* – see page 45
* *Pleioblastus variegatus* – see page 46
* *Pleioblastus viridistriatus* – see page 47

Medium displays in containers
* *Fargesia murielae* – see page 37
* *Phyllostachys nigra* – see page 43
* *Thamnocalamus tessellatus* – see page 53

Tall and dominant displays in containers
* *Bambusa multiplex* 'Alphonso-Karrii' – see page 32
* *Fargesia dracocephala* – see page 36
* *Fargesia nitida* – see page 37
* *Fargesia robusta* – see page 38
* *Fargesia utilis* – see page 38
* *Phyllostachys aurea* – see page 41
* *Pseudosasa japonica* – see page 48
* *Semiarundinaria fastuosa* – see page 51
* *Semiarundinaria yashadake kimmei* – see page 51
* *Shibataea kumasaca* – see page 52
* *Thamnocalamus crassinodus* – see page 52
* *Thamnocalamus spathiflorus* – see page 53

Creating a Japanese-style bamboo garden

Do these suit small gardens?

Japanese-style designs are ideal for a small garden, where they create quiet, restful areas for contemplation. Their simplicity of design, usually with raked gravel crossed by stepping stones, belies the dedication and attention to detail their success demands. Background screens of bamboos, as well as plants in containers, help to create memorable and distinctive gardens. Oriental-style features can be added to the design, but ensure they are not dominant.

ASSESSING THE AREA

Preferably, a small Japanese garden needs to be flat. This ensures that gravel does not slowly move downhill. However, where a garden is sloped, terracing is a solution, often enabling clumps of non-invasive bamboos to be planted between the levels. Alternatively, if the garden has a long, shallow slope, level off an area at the base – or one-third up the slope – and sculpt the slopes into areas that flow gently into and out of it (see opposite page).

DESIGN FOR A FLAT AREA

Within a gravelled area, perennial weeds and ineffective drainage are the main problems. Therefore, during construction work dig out all perennial weeds and install land drains, either formed of perforated 7.5 cm (3 in) wide plastic tubing or clay pipes. It is essential to rake the soil level and to firm it by systematically shuffling sideways across the entire area. Then, rake the area and lay a permeable membrane over it to prevent the growth of weeds.

Where 'ground-planted' bamboos are to be used in the design, first plant them in a container which can be buried in the soil so that its rim is about 5 cm (2 in) above the surface. The weed-preventing membrane can be cut around it. Planting bamboos in containers and using them in this way prevents them spreading and sending up shoots through the membrane.

Where stepping stones are needed, these must next be put into position; their spacing and positions are influenced by the area and the direction from which people enter and leave. Natural-looking paving slabs are desirable but expensive, and an alternative is a medley of differently sized large stones. Thin slabs of tree trunks can be used but are slippery in wet weather. Rather than creating just one path – which gives the impression that the area is cut in half – where possible use two sets of stepping stones that unite.

Sometimes, large rocks are used to depict meditative islands, with the gravel raked to create an impression of water. However, in a small area this is difficult to replicate.

When the stepping stones are in position, spread gravel around them, so that its surface is fractionally below the surfaces of the stepping stones.

Large rocks

Ground-planted bamboos – container rims 5 cm (2 in) above surface

Cobbles

Stepping stones

Raked gravel

Permeable membrane

Soil

Land drain

Possible ornamental additions

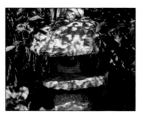

Stone lantern

Bamboo deer scarer

DESIGNS FOR A SLOPING AREA

Deciduous trees

Bamboo

Bamboo

Stream

Japanese Maple

Japanese Maple

Raked gravel

Large rocks

A slight slope above a flat and gravelled area is ideal for a woodland garden formed of deciduous trees and evergreen conifers. *Acer* spp. (Japanese Maples), with their colourful, finely divided leaves, create a sympathetic feature, especially when combined with water splashing from one pool to another. Where deciduous trees are used, position tall ones about 6 m (20 ft) above the flat area so that in autumn fallen leaves do not create a problem. Lower-growing ornamental maples are less trouble and can be planted nearer the gravel.

EDGINGS

To restrict the spread of gravel, use edging that harmonizes with the feature, such as wide bamboo canes protruding 13–15 cm (5–6 in) above it. Vertical log sections are an alternative – but they must have a clinical rather than rustic quality.

Edgings formed of wide bamboo canes empathize with Japanese-style surroundings.

SCREENS

Screens and fences must have an oriental appearance Lightweight screens formed of bamboo canes closely secured together with wires and up to 1.8 m (6 ft) high are ideal as backgrounds, but are not strong enough as boundaries. For these, a more functional design is needed, but there is always the possibility of erecting an bamboo screen 90 cm–1.2 m (3–4 ft) from the boundary. This space enables the boundary fence to be maintained. Positioning a cloaking screen close to an entrance also helps to maintain the illusion of an oriental garden.

These cloaked entrances, known as 'spirit walls', are used to deflect evil spirits from entering a garden, thereby preserving peace and encouraging good influences within a garden.

Screens formed of bamboo canes held in a framework create attractive backgrounds.

Pebble streams

Pebbles, as well as coloured slate, can be used to create the illusion of streams. They are especially useful when you are visually uniting a slope with a flat area. Add irregularly shaped paving slabs as stepping stones across the 'stream' to add to the impression of a stream.

RELIGIOUS INFLUENCE

Early Japanese gardens were partly influenced by Shintoism, a religion that sees humans, animals, plants and all natural things as equals and to be respected, both collectively and individually. Gardens designed with these principles in mind have meticulously formed and maintained natural-looking scenes, to reflect the beauty of nature. They generate an atmosphere of contemplation, peace and tranquillity.

CONTAINER OPPORTUNITIES

Bamboos growing in containers are ideal features in Japanese gardens. The range of suitable bamboos is wide, and many are recommended on page 13.

Bamboos as feature plants

How can I use them to best effect?

Bamboos can be used in many ways, but look superb planted in borders (pages 10–11). It is also possible to use just one or two distinctive bamboos in strategic positions that enable them immediately to capture attention. Some bamboos are prized for their colourful canes or foliage and create dramatic features. If space is limited, you can grow bamboos in containers (pages 12–13) and position them in gardens with a range of different and distinctive styles.

MATCHING VIGOUR WITH POSITION

Unlike trees, which are bought when small and may eventually outgrow their allotted positions, clump-forming bamboos spread quite slowly. Rampant types, of course, are likely to spread, but those with a moderately vigorous nature can be controlled (see pages 24–25). Vigorous types are best reserved for dramatic features in a woodland or wildlife garden. The vigour of the species in the A–Z of bamboos (pages 32–55) is clearly indicated to help you.

Bamboos can be used in a garden to create striking features, perhaps alongside a natural stream (but not streams formed with a flexible liner). When choosing a bamboo for a position near a gate, select one with a relatively upright habit, such as *Fargesia murielae* or *Fargesia nitida*. In a circular bed in a lawn, however, the arching, leaf-packed canes of *Chusquea culeou* create a more dramatic display.

In a corner bed at the edge of a lawn, bamboos with coloured canes, such as *Phyllostachys nigra* (Black-stemmed Bamboo), produce magnificent displays, especially when they can be seen close up and in full sun. Bamboos with colourful canes are featured on page 22.

Where bamboos can be positioned close to a firm surface – a path, patio or terrace – species with colourful leaves are ideal; many of these are described on page 23. The leaves can then be admired close up and throughout the year. The range of bamboos to choose from is impressively wide.

Phyllostachys aurea *(Fishpole Bamboo) has canes that have a distinctive swelling at each of their joints.*

Chusquea culeou *has attractive canes and clusters of mid-green leaves resembling those of a 'bottle-brush' plant.*

Fargesia murielae *(Umbrella Bamboo) has a graceful and arching habit, together with attractive leaves and canes.*

Fargesia murielae *'Simba' is lower-growing than the species (see left) and is ideal for planting in containers on patios.*

Wind, rain and snow

Bamboos such as *Chusquea* have canes with masses of small leaves, which sway in strong winds. If you plant them in a restricted position, such as next to a drive or a footpath, they may block it. The canes tend to splay outwards when drenched with rain. After snow falls, and before it can be removed, the canes become weighed down and may completely obstruct nearby paths.

Creating a Mediterranean aura

Although bamboos do not have a Mediterranean heritage, they can be mixed with other plants to create a warm, balmy and sun-rich aura. Clearly, appropriate settings are not available in all temperate zones, so you may need to set up a small, wind-sheltered area that will protect plants with Mediterranean origins. The choice of plants is wide; some have the bonus of aromatic leaves and are, occasionally, accompanied by richly fragrant flowers.

Are bamboos suitable?

BAMBOOS IN MEDITERRANEAN SETTINGS

Clusters of variously sized containers can be used to create attractive features for patios and terraces.

Above: Strategically placed containers can create privacy and slight shade on patios.

Left: Plants in containers introduce much-needed height to patios and water features.

PLANTS WITH A MEDITERRANEAN AURA

Plants with attractive foliage include the temperate-hardy *Trachycarpus fortunei* (Chusan Palm) and *Chamaerops humilis* (Dwarf Fan Palm) (pages 74–75), yuccas, many grasses (pages 62–71), *Cordyline*, *Eucalyptus*, *Fatsia japonica*, *Phormium tenax* and its many forms, *Pittosporum* and bamboos.

Additionally, there are many evergreen flowering shrubs that help to conjure a warm, Mediterranean ambience; these include rosemary, *Choisya ternata*, lavender, *Salvia officinalis*, *Brachyglottis* 'Sunshine', *Carpenteria californica*, *Cistus* and *Olearia*.

Where a Mediterranean garden merges with a patio or terrace, bamboos growing in pots and tubs create dramatic features. There are many species to choose from – in a range of heights – and these are featured on page 13.

Patios overflowing with potted plants are a common sight in Mediterranean regions. Group your potted plants around pots or tubs of bamboos, but take care not to cloak ornamental containers.

SCENTED PLANTS

Many plants with a Mediterranean aura have aromatic leaves. Here are a few to consider:

- *Aloysia triphylla* (Lemon-scented Verbena) – lemon.

- *Artemisia absinthium* (Common Wormwood) – sharp, with a hint of absinthe.

- *Choisya ternata* (Mexican Orange Blossom) – orange.

- *Cistus ladanifer* (Common Gum Cistus) – gum, with a hint of balsam.

- *Lavandula angustifolia* (English Lavender) – lavender.

- *Olearia macrodonta* (Daisy Bush) – strongly musk.

- *Rosmarinus officinalis* (Rosemary) – rosemary.

- *Salvia officinalis* (Sage) – bitter and pungent.

- *Santolina chamaecyparissus* (Cotton Lavender) – chamomile.

- *Thymus* x *citriodorus* (Lemon Thyme) – lemon.

- *Thymus herba-barona* (Caraway Thyme) – caraway.

- *Thymus vulgaris* (Common Thyme) – slightly sweet, pungent and spicy.

Windbreaks, hedges and screens

Can I create a bamboo hedge?

Several bamboos are suitable for forming functional and unusual hedges, as well as handsome screens and windbreaks. They decrease the wind's speed and help to create a more congenial area for other plants. Bamboos' 50–60 per cent permeability makes them ideal for this purpose – far better than solid screens such as brick walls or boarded fences, which result in strong eddies on their lee sides that may cause damage to nearby plants.

SELECTING SUITABLE BAMBOOS

Whether bamboos are planted primarily as a screen, hedge or windbreak, they all fulfil the role of creating an attractive background. But it is only the toughest and most resilient bamboos that are suitable for planting as a windbreak, and their ability to perform under such conditions very much depends on the exposed nature of the site.

Some of the *Phyllostachys* species are ideal as hedges but, because of their open natures, are not suitable as screens unless they are planted to form a wide hedge, which only works in large gardens.

Above: Fargesia murielae *(Umbrella Bamboo) is ideal for creating a background screen or to separate one part of a garden from another.*
Left: Thamnocalmus spathiflorus *is clump-forming, non-invasive and good for creating an attractive screen of pale green leaves.*

Because bamboos sometimes die after flowering, it is best to plant a hedge formed of several different species. Then, should flowering occur (see page 11), the hedge will not be a complete disaster. Even if flowered species do eventually recover, they are usually unsightly for several years. Therefore, if possible use a mixture of bamboo species.

MIXING SPECIES

As individual species of bamboos flower at irregular intervals, it is impossible to determine when flowering will next occur. However, it may well be worth talking to a knowledgeable local bamboo nursery, explaining your intention to create a hedge and asking when the species you desire last flowered in your area.

PLANTING EXAMPLES

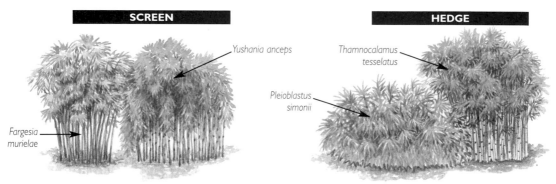

SCREEN

Yushania anceps

Fargesia murielae

HEDGE

Thamnocalamus tesselatus

Pleioblastus simonii

Creating privacy, especially in small or even moderately small gardens, is often essential, and these two species are perfect.

Hedges formed of bamboos, either internally or along boundaries, create distinctive features as well as effective barriers.

CHOICE GUIDE

Screen

- *Fargesia murielae* is graceful and elegant, with arching canes. It is clump-forming and non-invasive.

- *Yushania anceps* is superb, forming a tall and attractive background. It is spreading and invasive.

Hedge

- *Pleioblastus simonii* forms an attractive hedge, with upright canes. It is invasive.

- *Thamnocalamus tessellatus* is ideal as a relaxed and informal hedge. It is clump-forming and non-invasive.

Windbreak

- *Fargesia nitida* is hardy and even if it is partially denuded by winter winds invariably recovers and creates a new screen of attractive leaves. It is clump-forming and non-invasive.

- *Pseudosasa japonica* is ideal for creating a windbreak. It is tolerant of strong wind, as well as coastal salt spray, which tends to 'burn' the foliage of many bamboos. It is moderately invasive but easily checked.

- *Semiarundinaria fastuosa* is good as a windbreak, but its height can be stunted when it is planted in an exposed position. It is moderately invasive but easily checked.

OTHER HEDGING AND SCREENING BAMBOOS

- *Fargesia dracocephala* – see page 36 (clump-forming and non-invasive).

- *Fargesia robusta* – see page 38 (clump-forming and non-invasive).

- *Phyllostachys aurea* (and its forms) – see page 41 (moderately invasive but easily checked).

- *Phyllostachys nigra* (and its forms) – see page 43 (moderately invasive but easily checked).

- *Pleioblastus chino* – see page 44 (invasive nature).

- *Pseudosasa amabilis* – see page 47 (moderately invasive but easily checked).

Dangerous borders

Do not plant a bamboo hedge directly on the border line between your garden and that of a neighbour. The bamboo will spread and may cause inconvenience and annoyance. Instead, plant it at least 90 cm (3 ft) from the boundary.

RESTRAINING THE SPREAD OF BAMBOO HEDGES

A number of bamboos – with the exception of the clump-forming ones – have an aggressive, spreading nature, which may cause trouble. These are the ones described as 'invasive' throughout this book. This tendency to spread is not usually a problem when such bamboos are planted as a screen or windbreak, because adequate space is usually allowed for them, but when it comes to hedges the invasive nature of some bamboos can be quite tricky.

The best way to prevent an invasive bamboo spreading uncontrollably is simply not to plant it in the first place. However, if you have inherited a particularly vigorous species, either as a hedge or in a border, when moving to a new house and garden, dig a trench 30 cm (1 ft) deep and a spade width alongside it and remove all the soil. If the bamboo's rhizomes (roots) have yet to reach that point, fill the trench with easily removed material such as bark chippings. If, however, the rhizomes have reached that position, chop them off and remove them. Thereafter, each winter you should remove the bark chippings, chop off the rhizomes and replace the infill material.

Alternatively, you could install a metal barrier, as described on pages 24–25.

Do bamboo hedges need clipping?

If a clump-forming species has been planted, the only reason for 'pruning' is to limit the hedge's height. This can be done when a cane grows above the desired height. Do not put off cutting the canes until they are exceptionally tall. Old canes can also be cut out at their base.

Rather than resorting to clipping, however, it is better to select a bamboo that grows to the desired height.

Planting a bamboo hedge

For details, see page 29.

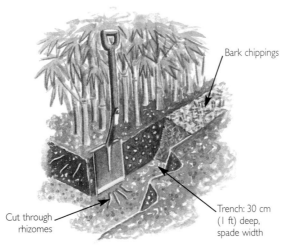

Bark chippings

Cut through rhizomes

Trench: 30 cm (1 ft) deep, spade width

Annually cutting back invasive rhizomes (roots) helps to prevent them trespassing into neighbouring gardens

Bamboos for ground cover

Are there low-growing bamboos?

Many bamboos cloak the soil beneath them in leaves and canes to produce an attractive feature. These are usually bamboos with an invasive and spreading nature, and they will soon colonize whole areas in gardens. Many are able to stabilize soil and prevent erosion caused by wind and rain. They are robust and, once established, will need little attention. These are intrusive bamboos; therefore do not plant them too close to a neighbour's garden.

GROUND COVER FOR ALL PLACES

Bamboos are versatile; the lists of bamboos on the opposite page indicate those that thrive in shade or cold areas, wet or dry positions, and in soil that needs to be stabilized. Before selecting a ground-cover bamboo, check the lists opposite to make sure it is suitable for the conditions in your garden.

Wherever a bamboo is positioned, it is essential to ensure thorough planting and during the first year to encourage rapid establishment (ways to tackle these tasks are detailed on pages 28–29).

The variegated and dwarf Sasa veitchii *creates a very pleasing feature when it is planted near to a path.*

Inserting posts in clumps of Plcioblastus variegatus *will encourage the presence of birds in the garden.*

SELECTING GROUND-COVER BAMBOOS

A wide range of bamboos is suitable for creating attractive ground cover, and many of them are illustrated here. They are also illustrated and fully described in the A–Z of bamboos (pages 32–55).

Indocalamus latifolius – see page 40

Indocalamus tessellatus – see page 40

Pleioblastus humilis var. pumilis – see page 45

Pleioblastus pygmaeus – see page 45

Pleioblastus variegatus – see page 46

Sasa palmata – see page 48

Sasa palmata nebulosa – see page 49

Sasa veitchii – see page 49

Sasaella masamuneana 'Albostriata' – see page 50

Sasaella ramosa – see page 50

Shibataea kumasaca – see page 52

Further bamboos

Indocalamus longiauritus: see page 55.
Sasa kurilensis (dwarf form): see page 55.
Sasa tsuboiana: see page 55.

MATCHING BAMBOOS TO SOIL AND SITE

BAMBOOS THAT GROW IN SHADE

- *Chimonobambusa marmorea* – see page 33
- *Chimonobambusa quadrangularis* – see page 33
- *Fargesia nitida* – see page 37
- *Indocalamus tessellatus* – see page 40
- *Pleioblastus simonii* – see page 46

- *Pseudosasa japonica* – see page 48
- *Sasa palmata* – see page 48
- *Sasa palmata nebulosa* – see page 49
- *Sasa tsuboiana* – see page 55
- *Sasa veitchii* – see page 49

HARDY BAMBOOS FOR COLD AREAS

- *Fargesia dracocephala* – see page 36
- *Fargesia murielae* – see page 37
- *Fargesia nitida* – see page 37
- *Indocalamus tessellatus* – see page 40
- *Phyllostachys nigra* (and its forms) – see page 43
- *Pleioblastus chino* – see page 44
- *Pleioblastus pygmaeus* – see page 45

- *Pleioblastus simonii* – see page 46
- *Pleioblastus variegatus* – see page 46
- *Pseudosasa japonica* – see page 48
- *Sasa palmata nebulosa* – see page 49
- *Semiarundinaria fastuosa* – see page 51
- *Shibataea kumasaca* – see page 52
- *Yushania anceps* – see page 54

BAMBOOS FOR STABILIZING BANKS

Bamboos are ideal for stabilizing banks, perhaps alongside streams. However, although many species appreciate damp conditions, they should not be planted with their roots in water or where the soil is permanently waterlogged. Other bamboos tolerate drier conditions, at least for a short while, and only then after they are well established. A couple of bamboos, *Pseudosasa japonica* and *Sasa palmata nebulosa*, have the ability to grow in both moist and dry conditions.

Bamboos for wet areas

- *Arundinaria gigantea tecta* – see page 32 (moderately invasive but easily checked)

- *Chimonobambusa quadrangularis* – see page 33 (invasive)

- *Chimonobambusa tumidissinoda* – see page 34 (clump-forming but invasive and spreading)

- *Pseudosasa japonica* – see page 48 (moderately invasive but easily checked)

- *Sasa palmata nebulosa* – see page 49 (invasive)

- *Shibataea kumasaca* – see page 52 (moderately invasive but easily checked)

Bamboos for dry positions

These bamboos will not grow on continually dry banks. Planting them in dry conditions will require regular watering until they are fully established.

- *Chusquea culeou* – see page 34 (clump-forming)

- *Pseudosasa japonica* – see page 48 (moderately invasive but easily checked)

- *Sasa palmata nebulosa* – see page 49 (invasive)

- *Sasa veitchii* – see page 49 (invasive)

- *Sasaella ramosa* – see page 50 (invasive)

Bamboos with colourful canes

<table>
<tr><td>

How colourful are bamboo canes?

</td><td>

Many bamboos have coloured canes. Some, such as *Chimonobambusa quadrangularis* (Square-stemmed Bamboo), have dark green, square-shaped canes. *Phyllostachys aurea* has distinctive, knobble-jointed canes that are a soft yellow when viewed in strong sunlight. Perhaps the most dramatic example, however, is *Phyllostachys nigra* (Black-stemmed Bamboo), which has canes that become jet black. It is ideal for planting in a 'mixed' border.

</td></tr>
</table>

COLOURFUL CANES

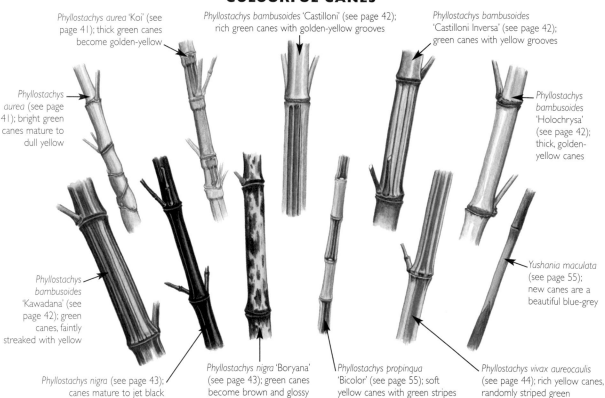

Phyllostachys aurea 'Koi' (see page 41); thick green canes become golden-yellow

Phyllostachys bambusoides 'Castilloni' (see page 42); rich green canes with golden-yellow grooves

Phyllostachys bambusoides 'Castilloni Inversa' (see page 42); green canes with yellow grooves

Phyllostachys aurea (see page 41); bright green canes mature to dull yellow

Phyllostachys bambusoides 'Holochrysa' (see page 42); thick, golden-yellow canes

Phyllostachys bambusoides 'Kawadana' (see page 42); green canes, faintly streaked with yellow

Yushania maculata (see page 55); new canes are a beautiful blue-grey

Phyllostachys nigra (see page 43); canes mature to jet black

Phyllostachys nigra 'Boryana' (see page 43); green canes become brown and glossy

Phyllostachys propinqua 'Bicolor' (see page 55); soft yellow canes with green stripes

Phyllostachys vivax aureocaulis (see page 44); rich yellow canes, randomly striped green

IDEAS FOR USING BAMBOOS WITH COLOURFUL CANES

The thick, colourful canes of Phyllostachys vivax *create an eye-catching feature.*

The blue-grey new canes of Yushania maculata *look great behind a curved bench.*

Few bamboos are as striking or dominant as Phyllostachys nigra, *with jet-black canes.*

Bamboos with colourful leaves

A few bamboos have leaves that are all-green, but many have colourful markings that bring additional colour to gardens and containers. Some bamboos, such as *Pleioblastus viridistriatus*, have leaves that are predominantly a bright colour, while others have striped leaves. These include *Pseudosasa japonica* 'Akebonosuji' and *Phyllostachys bambusoides* 'Castillonii Variegata'. A range of bamboos with attractively shaped or coloured leaves is shown below.

Are all bamboo leaves green?

COLOURFUL AND ATTRACTIVELY SHAPED LEAVES

Chimonobambusa marmurea (see page 33); attractive bright green leaves

Chusquea culeou (see page 34); often has a bottle-brush appearance

Fargesia murielae (see page 37); narrow, dark green leaves

Fargesia nitida (see page 37); narrow, bright green leaves

Hibanobambusa tranquillans 'Shiroshima' (see page 39); large, striped leaves

Indocalamus tessellatus (see page 40); exceptionally large and attractive leaves

Phyllostachys bambusoides 'Castilloni Variegata' (see page 42); green leaves are striped white

Phyllostachys bambusoides 'Kawadana' (see page 42); leaves are beautifully striped

Pleioblastus viridistriatus (see page 47); golden variegated leaves with pea-green stripes

Pseudosasa japonica 'Akebonosuji' (see page 48); most leaves are striped creamy-white

Sasa veitchii (see page 49); rich green leaves with white, often withered, edges

Sasaella masumuncana 'Albostriata' (see page 50); white stripes on young leaves

IDEAS FOR USING BAMBOOS WITH COLOURFUL LEAVES

Fargesia nitida *(right)* and Pleioblastus variegatus *(far left)* in a small group.

Pleioblastus viridistriatus *is small enough to be planted in a rock garden.*

Sasaella masamuneana *can be planted alongside paths, but constrain its roots.*

Invasive bamboos

Are all bamboos invasive?

Bamboos can be grouped according to their natural growth habit, whether clump-forming or aggressively invasive. Some are only moderately invasive and can be restrained when grown in a garden. It is essential that bamboos do not invade a neighbour's garden or puncture a liner in a garden pond. There is also the risk of young shoots damaging soft-skinned swimming pools, which may wholly or partly rest on the surface of the soil.

CLUMP-FORMING	INVASIVE

Fargesia nitida *'Nymphenburg' is a clump-forming and non-invasive bamboo that will not make a nuisance of itself.*

Hibanobambusa tranquillans *'Shiroshima' has an invasive nature and soon spreads over a wide area. Its spread may need to be restrained where space is not available for long-term growth.*

CONSTRAINING INVASIVE BAMBOOS

In their native habitats, bamboos can be left to form clumps or to wander and spread at will. In gardens, however, it may be necessary to restrict invasive types by burying a rust-proof barrier around them, or near to the garden's boundary. A barrier at least 50 cm (20 in) deep is necessary, with its top protruding about 7.5 cm (3 in) above the soil's surface. Alternatively, where the garden is large enough, dig a 50–60 cm (20–24 in) deep ditch along the boundary and keep it free from invasive and spreading roots, which botanically are known as rhizomes.

Where invasive bamboos are used to bind soil on a bank or steep slope, do not dig ditches across them as this may destabilize the soil. Instead, block the travels of the

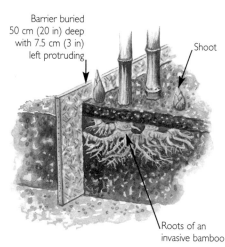

Barrier buried 50 cm (20 in) deep with 7.5 cm (3 in) left protruding

Shoot

Roots of an invasive bamboo

Although it is a time-consuming task to install a root barrier around a bamboo, this will prevent problems arising later (see opposite for details).

rhizomes with a sheet of non-ferrous metal buried to a depth of at least 50 cm (20 in).

A further way to restrain the roots is to chop off young shoots as soon as they appear above the soil. This will help to prevent the bamboo's spread, but is only really a temporary remedy and not a total solution. If a neighbour does not have a garden pond or soft-skinned swimming pool, however, there is little to worry about regarding invasive rhizomes and shoots.

Apart from invasive bamboos intruding on a neighbour's garden, rampant types could soon create a jungle in your own garden if they are planted too close to other bamboos or in a border with shrubs and other plants. Selecting bamboos with the right vigour is vital.

INSTALLING A BARRIER

This can be easily achieved and is best performed before planting bamboos, as it eliminates the necessity to retrample over the bed.

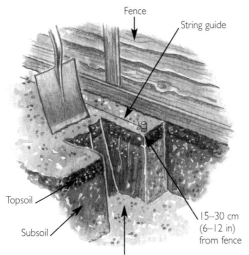

1 *Dig a narrow trench at least 50 cm (20 in) deep and 15–30 cm (6–12 in) from the fence. This reduces the risk of knocking your knuckles on the fence. Keep the topsoil and subsoil separate, so that they can be replaced in their earlier layers.*

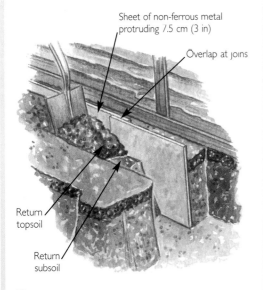

2 *Insert a sheet of non-ferrous metal into the trench, so that the top of the metal is 7.5 cm (3 in) above the surface. Then, replace and firm the soil. The soil will have bulked up but this will later settle.*

SELECTING THE RIGHT BAMBOO

As a guide to the selection of the right bamboo for your garden, the bamboos featured below are grouped according to their spreading nature. All of them are described in the A–Z of bamboos (pages 32–55).

CLUMP-FORMING AND NON-INVASIVE

- *Bambusa multiplex* 'Alphonso-Karrii' – see page 32
- *Chusquea culeou* – see page 34
- *Chusquea quila* – see page 35
- *Chusquea valdiviensis* – see page 36
- *Fargesia dracocephala* – see page 36
- *Fargesia murielae* – see page 37
- *Fargesia nitida* – see page 37
- *Fargesia robusta* – see page 38
- *Fargesia utilis* – see page 38
- *Thamnocalamus crassinodus* – see page 52
- *Thamnocalamus spathiflorus* – see page 53
- *Thamnocalamus tessellatus* – see page 53

MODERATELY INVASIVE BUT EASILY CHECKED

- *Arundinaria gigantea* – see page 32
- *Chusquea culeou* 'Tenuis' – see page 35
- *Hibanobambusa tranquillans* – see page 39
- *Phyllostachys aurea* – see page 41
- *Phyllostachys bambusoides* – see page 42
- *Phyllostachys bambusoides* 'Castilloni' – see page 42
- *Phyllostachys edulis* – see page 43
- *Phyllostachys nigra* – see page 43
- *Phyllostachys vivax* – see page 44
- *Pleioblastus viridistriatus* – see page 47
- *Pseudosasa amabilis* – see page 47
- *Pseudosasa japonica* – see page 48
- *Sasa tsuboiana* – see page 55
- *Semiarundinaria fastuosa* – see page 51
- *Semiarundinaria yashadake kimmei* – see page 51
- *Shibataea kamasaca* – see page 52

INVASIVE

- *Chimonobambusa marmorea* – see page 33
- *Chimonobambusa quadrangularis* – see page 33
- *Chimonobambusa tumidissinoda* – see page 34
- *Hibanobambusa tranquillans* 'Shiroshima' – see page 39
- *Indocalamus latifolius* – see page 40
- *Indocalamus tessellatus* – see page 40
- *Pleioblastus chino* – see page 44
- *Pleioblastus humilis* var. *pumilis* – see page 45
- *Pleioblastus pygmaeus* – see page 45
- *Pleioblastus simonii* – see page 46
- *Pleioblastus variegatus* – see page 46
- *Sasa palmata* – see page 48
- *Sasa palmata nebulosa* – see page 49
- *Sasa veitchii* – see page 49
- *Sasaella masamuneana* 'Albostriata' – see page 50
- *Sasaella ramosa* – see page 50
- *Yushania anceps* – see page 54
- *Yushania anceps* 'Pitt White' – see page 54

How high do bamboos grow?

Are bamboos always very large?

Bamboos encompass everything from pygmy-sized types to robust species that grow up to 12 m (40 ft) or more tall. The eventual height of a bamboo is influenced not only by its species but also by the amount of rainfall and temperature throughout the growing season in the local climate. Cold and strong winds reduce the length of the bamboo's growing period each year, thereby also reducing its growth and ultimate height.

VARIATIONS IN HEIGHT

Bamboos grow taller in their native areas than in cool, temperate climates. When you are researching bamboo heights, therefore, check that the measurements relate to conditions in your area. Even within temperate regions, heights radically vary between sheltered and relatively warm areas and those that are more exposed.

Pleioblastus viridistriatus *grows 90 cm–1.2 m (3-4 ft) high and is ideal for planting in small gardens, as well as in containers on a patio or terrace.*

Phyllostachys bambusoides *grows up to 6 m (20 ft) high – sometimes more – and creates a dominant and dramatic feature.*

HEIGHTS AND PLANTING SCHEMES

Fargesia murielae

Sasaella masamuneana

Pleioblastus variegatus

Chusquea culeou

Hibanobambusa tranquillans 'Shiroshima'

Sasa palmata

Phyllostachys aurea *creates a distinctive feature when planted in a circular bed, perhaps in the centre of a patio.*

A medley of bamboos with different heights creates a dramatic feature in a border, especially if they also contrast in leaf size.

A moderately tall bamboo planted among low, ground-covering bamboos produces an attractive feature.

BAMBOO HEIGHTS AND CONTAINERS

Tall, with distinctive canes and foliage

Low-growing, with variegated leaves

Tall and low-growing bamboos can be grown in containers (see right for suitable plants).

Bamboos and the containers they are planted in should be in proportion (for a range of suitable bamboos for containers, see pages 12–13). Tall bamboos planted in containers are at risk of being blown over, especially when they are grown in exposed positions. They are therefore best placed in a sheltered corner.

CANE MATURITY

The width and height of an individual bamboo cane does not increase after its first year of growth. However, as each successive cane emerges from the same clump, its width and height are greater, and this continues until the optimum thickness and height for the canes of that species are reached. Canes mature at about three years old, and live for a further 10 or more years.

THICKNESS AND HEIGHT OF CANES

Bamboos in tropical regions are much faster-growing than those in temperate climates, where cane heights of 30 m (100 ft) and diameters of 20 cm (8 in) have been achieved in only one growing season.

CANES OR CULMS?

Culm is the botanical term for the hollow stems of grasses and especially used when referring to bamboos. It is often seen in books about bamboos and in plant catalogues.

RANGES IN HEIGHT

Bamboos listed in the A–Z of bamboos (pages 32–55) are here grouped according to height. These measurements relate to bamboos in temperate climates and can only be taken as approximate heights. Indeed, opinions about the heights of bamboos are wide-ranging.

SMALL BAMBOOS – UP TO 1.5 M (5 FT)

- *Indocalamus latifolius* – see page 40
- *Indocalamus tessellatus* – see page 40
- *Pleioblastus humilis* var. *pumilis* – see page 45
- *Pleioblastus pygmaeus* – see page 45
- *Pleioblastus variegatus* – see page 46
- *Pleioblastus viridistriatus* – see page 47
- *Sasa tsuboiana* – see page 55
- *Sasa veitchii* – see page 49
- *Sasaella masamuneana* 'Albostriata' – see page 50
- *Sasaella ramosa* – see page 50
- *Shibataea kumasaca* – see page 52

MEDIUM BAMBOOS – 1.5–3 M (5–10 FT)

- *Bambusa multiplex* 'Alphonso-Karrii' – see page 32
- *Chimonobambusa marmorea* – see page 33
- *Chimonobambusa quadrangularis* – see page 33
- *Chimonobambusa tumidissinoda* – see page 34
- *Chusquea culeou* 'Tenuis' – see page 35
- *Fargesia murielae* – see page 37
- *Phyllostachys nigra* – see page 43
- *Pleioblastus chino* – see page 44
- *Sasa palmata* – see page 48
- *Sasa palmata nebulosa* – see page 49

TALL BAMBOOS – 3–6 M (10–20 FT) OR MORE

- *Arundinaria gigantea* – see page 32
- *Chusquea culeou* – see page 34
- *Chusquea quila* – see page 35
- *Chusquea valdiviensis* – see page 36
- *Fargesia dracocephala* – see page 36
- *Fargesia nitida* – see page 37
- *Fargesia robusta* – see page 38
- *Fargesia utilis* – see page 38
- *Hibanobambusa tranquillans* – see page 39
- *Hibanobambusa tranquillans* 'Shiroshima' – see page 39
- *Phyllostachys aurea* – see page 41
- *Phyllostachys bambusoides* – see page 42
- *Phyllostachys bambusoides* 'Castilloni' – see page 42
- *Phyllostachys edulis* – see page 43
- *Phyllostachys vivax* – see page 44
- *Pleioblastus simonii* – see page 46
- *Pseudosasa amabilis* – see page 47
- *Pseudosasa japonica* – see page 48
- *Semiarundinaria fastuosa* – see page 51
- *Semiarundinaria yashadake kimmei* – see page 51
- *Thamnocalamus crassinodus* – see page 52
- *Thamnocalamus spathiflorus* – see page 53
- *Thamnocalamus tessellatus* – see page 53
- *Yushania anceps* – see page 54
- *Yushania anceps* 'Pitt White' – see page 54

Planting bamboos

Like all other garden plants, bamboos' planting must be thorough, with friable soil drawn over and firmed around the roots. Bamboos do not have deep roots, so digging the top 30 cm (1 ft) of soil, mixing in well-decomposed compost or manure and a dusting of slow-acting fertilizers, is usually all that is needed. If the drainage is poor, loosen the lower soil to ensure that water does not remain on the soil's surface, especially in winter when it might freeze.

GETTING THE TIMING RIGHT

The majority of bamboos sold by garden centres and nurseries are established and growing in containers. Occasionally they are sold as bare-rooted plants, but this is a rarity. The only time most home gardeners plant such material is when they are dividing congested bamboos in a garden.

CONTAINER-GROWN BAMBOOS

Like other container-grown plants, bamboos can be planted whenever the soil is workable, and the weather suitable. However, bamboos establish themselves more readily and with less disturbance when planted into warm, moist soil in late spring or early summer. This, of course, is not always possible, and the demand for 'instant' gardens means that planting occurs throughout summer and into early autumn. Step-by-step guidance to planting a container-grown bamboo is given on the right.

BARE-ROOTED BAMBOOS

Before the introduction of container-grown plants in the 1960s, bamboos were sold with bare roots covered in sacking to prevent drying. Recommended planting dates varied, from early spring for warm areas to late spring or early summer for cold regions. Bare-rooted bamboos rapidly establish when they are planted in warm, moisture-retentive soil.

As soon as you receive the plants (or after division of home-grown plants), place the roots in a bucket of tepid water for a couple of hours to ensure they are moist. Then, remove them and allow any excess water to drain.

Plant the rhizomes (roots) so that they are slightly deeper than before. This allows for soil settlement and keeps the rhizomes cooler. Draw and firm friable soil in layers over the roots. Firm it with the heel of a shoe. Then rake the surface level to remove footprints (see the opposite page for 'After planting' advice).

PLANTING FROM A CONTAINER

1 As soon as a container-grown bamboo is received, place the container on a well-drained surface and thoroughly water the compost. Several waterings may be necessary. Then, leave the plant in place until the following day. Unless the compost is evenly moist, the bamboo's establishment will be delayed.

2 Prepare the planting position (see above). Form and firm a slight mound in the base of the hole. Carefully remove the bamboo from the container and position the rootball in the hole. Rotate the plant so that its most attractive side faces the front of the border.

3 Check that the top of the soil ball is slightly below the level of the surrounding soil – use a straight-edged board to do this. Draw friable soil around the rootball and firm it in layers. Use the heel of a shoe to firm the soil. Lastly, level the surface to remove footprints.

4 Insert a label by the plant or record its position in a notebook. Then, thoroughly water the soil but do not create a muddy surface. Either use a watering-can with the rose turned upwards or a hosepipe with a nozzle that produces a fine mist.

AFTER PLANTING ...

- For up to two years after planting bamboos, regularly water the soil – from spring to autumn.
- Immediately after planting and watering them, form a 5 cm (2 in) thick mulch around plants to conserve soil moisture and to keep the roots cool, especially during hot summers. Young roots are soon damaged if they become dry.

- Where bare-rooted bamboos are planted, it may be necessary to support long canes with tall sticks or bamboo canes.
- In exposed and windy positions, erect a strong canvas or fine-mesh wire-netting screen on the windward side. This prevents leaves drying and roots being loosened in the soil if the canes are rocked and disturbed by the wind.

PLANTING A BAMBOO HEDGE

Bamboos are relatively surface-rooting, and therefore deep cultivation is usually unnecessary (see top of opposite page). For the best times to plant container-grown plants, see 'Container-grown bamboos' opposite. The best planting times for bare-rooted bamboos are given in 'Bare-rooted bamboos' opposite.

Dig a trench about 30 cm (1 ft) wide and 20–30 cm (8–12 in) deep, and lightly fork over the base to loosen the soil.

When you are planting clump-forming species, space the plants about 60 cm (2 ft) apart; closer planting produces a dense hedge more rapidly. It is cheaper to use plants with only two canes each, but these take longer to produce a dense hedge. As a guide to its development, a newly planted hedge will double its number of canes in the first season, then double that number during each ensuing season.

Another way to produce a hedge is to plant 15 cm (6 in) long pieces of rhizome about 15 cm (6 in) apart. Horizontally positioned rhizomes will produce roots quicker than vertically placed pieces, whereas vertical ones will develop shoots faster than horizontal pieces. Therefore, to create a hedge packed with roots and canes, alternate the rhizomes.

After planting, thoroughly water the soil and add a mulch. For about a year, ensure that the soil does not become dry.

Method 1: Containers

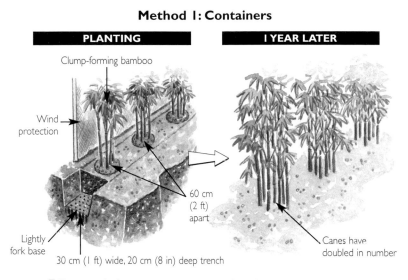

PLANTING | **I YEAR LATER**

Clump-forming bamboo

Wind protection

Lightly fork base

30 cm (1 ft) wide, 20 cm (8 in) deep trench

60 cm (2 ft) apart

Canes have doubled in number

↗ Planting a hedge using container-grown plants is more expensive than creating it from pieces of rhizomes (see below for details).

Method 2: Rhizomes

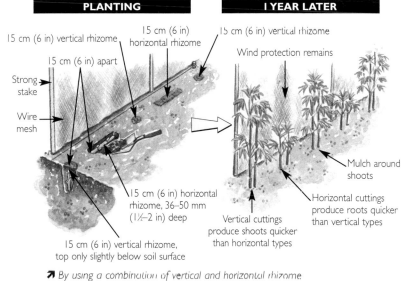

PLANTING | **I YEAR LATER**

15 cm (6 in) vertical rhizome

15 cm (6 in) horizontal rhizome

15 cm (6 in) apart

Strong stake

Wire mesh

15 cm (6 in) horizontal rhizome, 36–50 mm (1½–2 in) deep

15 cm (6 in) vertical rhizome, top only slightly below soil surface

15 cm (6 in) vertical rhizome

Wind protection remains

Mulch around shoots

Horizontal cuttings produce roots quicker than vertical types

Vertical cuttings produce shoots quicker than horizontal types

↗ By using a combination of vertical and horizontal rhizome cuttings, a stout bamboo hedge can be created within 3–4 years.

Looking after and increasing bamboos

Do they need regular attention?

Like all plants, it is important to get bamboos established quickly after planting or division. Regular watering, especially during their early years, is vital, as are mulching and feeding. Occasionally, old canes need to be removed and, during winter, snow brushed off before it freezes, weighs down the canes and causes permanent damage. A soft-bristled sweeping brush, with a handle 1.5–1.8 m (5–6 ft) long, is useful for removing light coverings of snow.

LOOKING AFTER BAMBOOS

Bamboos are resilient plants and need little attention, but a small amount of extra care can produce even better results.

- **Feeding:** In spring, just as growth begins, dust a high-nitrogen fertilizer around clumps. Thoroughly but lightly water in the fertilizer.
- **Mulching:** After feeding and watering in spring, form a yearly mulch around clumps. A range of mulches can be used, including well-decomposed garden compost or manure. This helps to keep the soil moist and cool, as well as providing additional food.
- **Watering:** Thorough but light applications of water are essential until plants are fully established, and especially during periods of drought in bamboos' early years.

BEFORE	AFTER

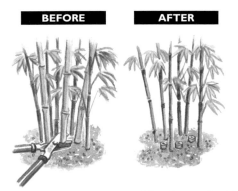

Occasionally, in spring some of the old canes should be cut out, at their bases, to reduce congestion.

- **Cutting out old and dead canes:** Cut old canes to ground level to keep clumps tidy. Tackle this task in spring before feeding and mulching. This pruning encourages a better circulation of air at the clump's base.
- **Restraining spread:** Periodically – and where necessary – use a sharp spade to sever and dig out spreading rhizomes.

MOVING ESTABLISHED BAMBOOS

This is best carried out in either early spring or early to mid-autumn. If bamboos are moved during their main growing season, the growth of young shoots will be retarded. If a large clump is being moved, this can be combined with reducing its size and removing young parts for replanting elsewhere.

Moving large bamboos can sometimes involve the efforts of several people. Here are the stages:

- If the clump contains masses of old canes, cut some of them out at ground level.
- Tie the rest of the canes together to prevent people being knocked in the face by them.
- There are two techniques used to move an established clump. The first is to dig a 60–75 cm (24–30 in) deep and 45 cm (18 in) wide trench around half of the plant. Then, dig under the roots, drawing soil back to the outer edge of the trench to create a ramp up which the clump can later be pulled. Slowly proceed to undercut the roots, and use a spade to cut around the edges of the clump. When the clump becomes insecure, put long planks under it and up the angled edge of the trench. Use sacking and ropes to hold a large clump together. The second way is to dig a wide trench about 45 cm (18 in) deep around the entire clump and then dig under it. This method is usually successful, but results in more damage to the roots.
- Prepare a planting hole that is wide and deep enough to accommodate the roots.
- If the clump has been manipulated on to a piece (or pieces) of strong sacking, it can be dragged or lifted into position in the new hole. Check that the depth is suitable (slightly deeper than before) and rotate the plant until its best side faces the main viewing position.
- Draw and firm friable soil over the roots, working it between them. Firm the soil in layers and not all at once.
- Dust the surface soil with a fertilizer, thoroughly water and apply a mulch around the plant.
- Keep the soil moist for up to a year.

INCREASING BAMBOOS

Raising new plants vegetatively – by dividing clumps, taking cane offsets or by cuttings of rhizomes (roots) – is achievable for most home gardeners. Sowing seeds is a slow method of growing new plants, but it does have the benefit of ensuring that the new plants will not produce flowers and seeds – then possibly die – within the lifetime of the sower. Details of the flowering nature of bamboos are provided on page 11.

Cane offsets

Division of clumps

➜ Lift and divide large clumps in spring, just as new growth is beginning. It is possible to use a spade to cut away a few shoots with the clump still in its position, but if the clump is large and several pieces are desired it is best to dig up the clump in its entirety. Large pieces can be moved to their new growing positions, and small ones either potted or planted into a nursery bed.

↗ In spring, cut these away from established clumps and either plant them into a new growing position or in a nursery bed. It may be necessary to support them with strong bamboo canes.

Rhizome cuttings

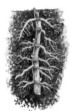

← This is an ideal propagative method for bamboos with a vigorous and spreading nature. It is also a less arduous method of propagation than division, but it takes longer to produce established plants. In mid-spring, lift a few roots (rhizomes) and cut them into sections 15–25 cm (6–10 in) long. Place them in pots of compost, with the topmost bud slightly above the surface. Water and place outdoors until late autumn; then, place in a warm greenhouse. Keep the compost lightly moist during winter and place outdoors in spring. Within two years they can be planted into a border. Incidentally, rhizome cuttings can also be used to create a hedge (see page 29).

BAMBOO TROUBLESHOOTING

Bamboos, especially those growing in temperate climates, are relatively free from pests and diseases. Dryness around the roots of newly planted bamboos, as well as those grown in containers, causes leaves and roots to shrivel. Therefore, regular watering during the first year is essential.

PROBLEM	DAMAGE	SOLUTION
Greenfly (aphids)	Greenfly suck soft leaves and shoot tips, causing distortion. Only occasionally a problem.	Usually, it is not worth spraying with an insecticide, unless plants are badly infected. Some species are more likely to be infested than others. With age, the foliage toughens and the problem diminishes.
Slugs and snails	They chew the young, soft parts of shoots; the damage is initially cloaked by the shoot's outer sheaf and often does not become apparent until later.	In wet springs and early summers, put baits around the bases of plants. Also, pick off and destroy slugs and snails (they are mostly seen at night).
Rabbits, squirrels and mice	They chew young shoots, often causing major problems for the health of the plant.	It is difficult to deter them. Fine-mesh wire-netting laid over the soil around bamboos sometimes deters mice when shoots are still underground, but long-term protection involves trapping and killing them. In law, rabbits and squirrels are protected, and any culling must be done humanely. The best solution is to call in a pest-control company.
Dogs and cats	Domestic animals dig and scratch the soil around shoots, especially if the soil is light and friable, and may damage them.	It is difficult to deter cats from using the area as a toilet, or dogs from burying bones, but placing wire-netting over the surface until the canes are established, and the soil consolidated and hardened, is a solution.
Bamboo mites	Mites cluster on the undersides of leaves, causing yellow and puckered areas.	Syringe entire plants with clean water, especially in hot and dry weather. If the attack is severe, cut off and burn infested leaves from strongly growing bamboos. Also use a systemic insecticide. Buy plants from reputable sources.

A–Z of bamboos

Many bamboos are suitable for gardens in temperate regions and 46 of them are described and illustrated here. In addition, 14 others are featured on page 55, together with two that are especially suitable for warm conservatories. Botanical names of many bamboos have been radically changed during recent years and therefore both up-to-date and earlier ones are included, together with common names, where applicable. Heights are indicated for each bamboo, but these vary depending on the age of the clump and the environment (see pages 26–27).

Arundinaria gigantea

Cane Reed (UK) **Canebreak Bamboo** (USA) **Giant Cane** (USA) **Giant Reed** (UK)
Southern Cane (USA) **Southern Canebreak** (USA) **Switch Cane** (USA)
Switch Reed (USA)

Vigorous bamboo, also known as *Arundinaria macrosperma*, *Arundinaria tecta* and *Bambusa newmanii*. It develops dull, yellowish-green canes, sometimes more than 6 m (20 ft) high in its native area, and up to 36 mm (1½ in) wide. The rather pale, soft green leaves are up to 35 cm (14 in) long and 2.5 cm (1 in) wide on old canes, but less on young ones and especially on plants in temperate climates, when they are usually 20 cm (8 in) long and 2.5 cm (1 in) wide. *Arundinaria gigantea tecta* is less vigorous, with small to medium, pale green leaves. It grows in damp soils.

Height: 4.5–6 m (15–20 ft), often more.

Spread/rootstock: Forms dense thickets. Moderately invasive, but easily checked.

Soil and situation: Fertile, moisture-retentive but well-drained soil in full sun or dappled shade. It is not suitable for cold areas.

Propagation: Division of clumps, cane offsets and rhizome cuttings (see page 31).

Native to: USA (mainly southern and southeastern states bordering the Gulf of Mexico).

Bambusa multiplex 'Alphonso-Karrii'

Alphonse Karr Bamboo (USA) **Hedge Bamboo** (UK/USA)
Oriental Hedge Bamboo (USA)

Also known as *Bambusa glaucescens* 'Alphonse Karr' and *Bambusa multiplex* 'Alphonse-Karr', this tender bamboo reveals bright yellow canes randomly marked with vivid green stripes. Sometimes, young canes have pink shading. The mid-green leaves are small and dainty, usually about 10 cm (4 in) long and 30 mm (1¼ in) wide.

Height: 1.8–3 m (6–10 ft), sometimes more.

Spread/rootstock: Clump-forming and non-invasive.

Soil and situation: Fertile, moisture-retentive but well-drained soil. In temperate climates it is best grown in a container, so that in cold winters it can be over-wintered in a greenhouse or conservatory. It can also be used as an indoor pot plant.

Propagation: Division of clumps and cane offsets (see page 31).

Native to: China.

Chimonobambusa marmorea

Also known as *Arundinaria marmorea* and *Bambusa marmorea*, this slightly tender bamboo develops canes up to 1.8 m (6 ft) high and 12 mm (½ in) wide. They are thick-walled, initially beige, later dull or deep purple when grown in full sunlight. The leaves, up to 15 cm (6 in) long and 12 mm (½ in) wide, are bright green.

Height: 1.5–1.8 m (5–6 ft), sometimes more.

Spread/rootstock: Spreading and invasive.

Soil and situation: Fertile, moisture-retentive but well-drained soil in full sun or dappled shade. It is not suitable for cold areas.

Propagation: Division of clumps and rhizome cuttings (see page 31).

Native to: Japan.

Native name: Kan-chiku.

Chimonobambusa quadrangularis

Square Bamboo (USA)
Square-stemmed Bamboo (UK/USA)

Also known as *Arundinaria quadrangularis*, *Bambusa quadrangularis* and *Tetragonocalamus angulatus*, this robust, moderate- to fast-growing hardy bamboo has square, dark green canes (with rounded corners) that with maturity turn brownish green and are occasionally splashed purple. These are up to 3 m (10 ft) high and 18 mm (¾ in) wide. The deep olive-green leaves are up to 23 cm (9 in) long and slightly more than 2.5 cm (1 in) wide. Although moderately dominant in temperate climates, in Taiwan it has been recorded at 9 m (30 ft) high.

Height: 2.4–3 m (8–10 ft), sometimes more.

Spread/rootstock: Spreading and invasive.

Soil and situation: Fertile, moisture-retentive but well-drained soil in full sun or light, dappled shade. It is not suitable for cold areas.

Propagation: Division of clumps, cane offsets and rhizome cuttings (see page 31).

Native to: Southeast China and Taiwan.

Native names: Shikakudake, Shiho-chiku.

Chimonobambusa tumidissinoda

Also known as *Qiongzhuea tumidinoda*, it has glossy, olive or sap-green canes with swollen joints that resemble spinning tops. The small, glossy, light green leaves, 10 cm (4 in) long and 12 mm (½ in) wide, are borne in elegant plumes, creating a fountain-like appearance. It is not always hardy and therefore is not suitable for very cold areas.

Height: 90 cm–2.4 m (3–8 ft), sometimes more.

Spread/rootstock: Clump-forming, but invasive and spreading.

Situation and soil: Full sun or light shade and fertile, moisture-retentive soil.

Propagation: Division of clumps and rhizome cuttings (see page 31).

Native to: China (northeast Yunnan and southwest Sichuan).

WALKING STICKS

Because of the swollen, knob-like joints on the canes they have been used to make walking sticks.

Chusquea culeou

Sometimes listed in catalogues as *Chusquea couleou*, this hardy, distinctive, variable and graceful bamboo has yellow-green to olive canes and small, mid-green leaves, up to 8 cm (3½ in) long and 6 mm (¼ in) wide, borne on short branches, which create a bottle-brush appearance. The canes, up to 5.4 m (18 ft) high and 36 mm (1½ in) thick, create a dominant feature.

Height: 3.6–5.4m (12–18 ft).

Spread/rootstock: Clump-forming and non-invasive.

Soil and situation: Fertile, moisture-retentive but well-drained soil in full sun and sheltered from cold, strong wind.

Propagation: Division of clumps and cane offsets (see page 31).

Native to: South America.

Chusquea culeou 'Tenuis'

Sometimes listed as *Chusquea breviglumis* or *Chusquea culeou* 'Breviglumis', this slightly tender bamboo has thick, yellowish-green canes and small, mid-green leaves, up to 8 cm (3½ in) long and 6 mm (¼ in) wide. The canes, up to about 1.8 m (6 ft) high and 36 mm (1½ in) thick, create a large, dominant bamboo that seldom fails to make an impressive display.

Height: 1.8–2.1 m (6–7 ft).

Spread/rootstock: Moderately invasive but easily checked.

Soil and situation: Fertile, moisture-retentive but well-drained soil in full sun and sheltered from cold, strong wind.

Propagation: Division of clumps, cane offsets and rhizome cuttings (see page 31).

Native to: South America.

Chusquea quila

Distinctive bamboo with thick, yellowish-green canes, up to 5.4 m (18 ft) tall and 12–18 mm (½–¾ in) wide, that are often curved, creating a clump with a bowl-shaped outline. The light green leaves, 5 cm (2 in) long and 6 mm (¼ in) wide, are attractive but borne sparsely.

Height: 3–5.4 m (10–18 ft).

Spread/rootstock: Clump-forming and non-invasive.

Soil and situation: Fertile, moisture-retentive but well-drained soil in full sun and sheltered from cold, strong wind.

Propagation: Division or clumps and cane offsets (see page 31).

Native to: South America.

Chusquea valdiviensis

This tender bamboo is listed by some botanists as *Chusquea ramosissima*, although others report them as two different species. Whatever botanists claim, it is clear that it is an attractive bamboo, with thick, pale green and radically arching canes, often from ground level. Its height varies, usually up to 4.5 m (15 ft), but sometimes much more. The leaves, 13 cm (5 cm) long and 12 mm (½ in) wide, are rich, dark green.

Height: 3–4.5 m (10–15 ft), often more.

Spread/rootstock: Clump-forming and non-invasive.

Soil and situation: Fertile, moisture-retentive but well-drained soil in full sun and sheltered from cold, strong wind.

Propagation: Division of clumps and cane offsets (see page 31).

Native to: South America.

Fargesia dracocephala

Hardy, with slender, yellowish-green canes that later assume tints of purplish-red, especially when in full sun. The narrow canes are up to 4.5 m (15 ft) high, while the mid-green leaves, 10 cm (4 in) long and about 12 mm (½ in) wide, are small and help to form an attractive screen or hedge.

Height: 3–4.5 m (10–15 ft).

Spread/rootstock: Clump-forming and non-invasive.

Soil and situation: Fertile, moisture-retentive but well-drained soil in full sun or light shade. It can be grown in a tub, but the soil must not be allowed to dry out. Therefore, put the container out of direct sun and strong winds, and water regularly.

Propagation: Division of clumps and cane offsets (see page 31).

Native to: China (Sichuan).

Fargesia murielae

Umbrella Bamboo (UK/USA)

Also known as *Arundinaria murielae* and *Sinarundinaria murielae*, this hardy, elegant, easily grown, graceful bamboo has arching, bright green canes that mature to dull yellow-green. They grow about 2.4 m (8 ft) high, but in old and established clumps to 4 m (13 ft); the canes are about 12 mm (½ in) wide. Although hardy, in cold areas it has a tendency to lose some of its foliage during winter. The narrowly oblong, dark green leaves, 7.5 cm (3 in) long and 12 mm (½ in) wide, resemble those of *Fargesia nitida*. There are several superb varieties, including the popular 'Simba', which is shorter and seldom exceeds 1.8 m (6 ft). It is ideal for planting in a container on a patio.

Height: 1.8–2.4 m (6–8 ft), often more.

Spread/rootstock: Clump-forming and non-invasive.

Soil and situation: Fertile, moisture-retentive but well-drained soil in full sun or light shade. It can be grown in a tub, but the soil must not be allowed to dry out. Therefore, position the container out of direct sun and strong winds, and water regularly. It is ideal for forming a decorative screen.

Propagation: Division of clumps and cane offsets (see page 31).

Native to: Central China.

Fargesia nitida

Fountain Bamboo (UK/USA)
Queen of the Arundinarias (UK/USA)

Also known as *Arundinaria nitida* and *Sinarundinaria nitida*, this fast-growing, hardy bamboo has purple stems covered with a waxy bloom. The canes are 3.6–4.5 m (12–15 ft) high and up to 18 mm (¾ in) wide. The narrow, bright green, lance-shaped leaves, 8 cm (3½ in) long and 12 mm (½ in) wide, rustle attractively in the wind. It is one of the most graceful of all bamboos and is superb as a screen or windbreak.

Height: 3.6–4.5 m (12–15 ft).

Spread/rootstock: Clump-forming and non-invasive.

Soil and situation: Fertile, moisture-retentive but well-drained soil in full sun or light shade. It can be grown in a tub, but the soil must not be allowed to dry out. Therefore, position the container out of direct sun and strong winds, and water regularly.

Propagation: Division of clumps and cane offsets (see page 31).

Native to: Central China.

PANDA FOOD

Fargesia nitida – together with *Fargesia japonica, Yushania anceps* and *Indocalamus tessellatus* – is one of the bamboos that provides shoots, stems and leaves for Giant Pandas.

Fargesia robusta

An especially attractive, hardy bamboo with slender, yellowish-green canes and small, glossy, green leaves, 13 cm (5 in) long and 18 mm (¾ in) wide. It is an ideal bamboo for planting as a focal point, where it shows off its graceful foliage.

Height: 3–3.6 m (10–12 ft).

Spread/rootstock: Clump-forming and non-invasive.

Soil and situation: Fertile, moisture-retentive but well-drained soil in full sun or light shade. It can be grown in a tub, but the soil must not be allowed to dry out. Therefore, position the container out of direct sun and strong winds, and water regularly. It is ideal as a screen or hedge.

Propagation: Division of clumps and cane offsets (see page 31).

Native to: China.

Fargesia utilis

Another hardy and distinctive bamboo from this genus, with pale green, arching canes, occasionally tinted purple at their tops. The canes grow up to 4.5 m (15 ft) high and are 12–18 mm (½–¾ in) wide – sometimes slightly taller and 2.5 cm (1 in) wide. The small, dark green leaves, 10 cm (4 in) long and 12 mm (½ in) wide, are attractive; often well-established clumps have canes that cascade.

Height: 3–4.5 m (10–15 ft).

Spread/rootstock: Clump-forming and non-invasive.

Soil and situation: Fertile, moisture-retentive but well-drained soil in full sun or light shade. It can be grown in a tub, but the soil must not be allowed to dry out. Therefore, position the container out of direct sun and strong winds, and water regularly.

Propagation: Division of clumps and cane offsets (see page 31).

Native to: China (Yunnan).

CURE FOR IMPOTENCE

Bamboos have often been associated with the erotic arts, and it is claimed that a hard, amber-like secretion (tabasheer) that forms between the nodes of some species is a cure for impotence.

Hibanobambusa tranquillans

Distinctive, hardy hybrid bamboo, thought to be a cross between *Phyllostachys* and *Sasa*, and also known as *Phyllostachys tranquillans* and *Semiarundinaria tranquillans*. It develops slender canes with large leaves, 23 cm (9 in) long and 42 mm (1¾ in) wide, that create an attractive feature during winter. The canes are variable in vigour and usually grow to 4.5 m (15 ft) high and 30 mm (1¼ in) wide.

Height: 2.4–4.5 m (8–15 ft).

Spread/rootstock: Moderately invasive, but easily checked.

Soil and situation: Fertile, moisture-retentive but well-drained soil in full sun or light shade.

Propagation: Division of clumps, cane offsets and rhizome cuttings (see page 31).

Native to: Japan.

Native name: Inyou-chikuzoku.

Hibanobambusa tranquillans 'Shiroshima'

Hardy form, thought to be a variety from a cross between *Phyllostachys* and *Sasa*. It develops slender to medium canes and large leaves, 23 cm (9 in) long and 42 mm (1¾ in) wide, attractively and conspicuously striped creamy-white and often appearing to have a pink shade when young. It is more vigorous than the species. The canes are variable in vigour and usually grow 2.4–4.5 m (8–15 ft) high and up to 30 mm (1¼ in) wide.

Height: 2.4–4.5 m (8–15 ft).

Spread/rootstock: Invasive and spreading.

Soil and situation: Fertile, moisture-retentive but well-drained soil in full sun or light shade.

Propagation: Division of clumps, cane offsets and rhizome cuttings (see page 31).

Native to: Japan.

Indocalamus latifolius

Hardy and vigorous bamboo, also known as *Arundinaria latifolia*, with slender, erect canes and large, broad leaves, often 25 cm (10 in) long and 5 cm (2 in) wide. The canes normally grow 50 cm–1 m (20 in–3½ ft) high, although in warm and moist climates this may be more.

Height: Up to about 1 m (3½ ft), sometimes more.

Spread/rootstock: Invasive.

Soil and situation: Fertile, moisture-retentive soil in light shade. It is ideal for creating attractive ground cover.

Propagation: Division of clumps and rhizome cuttings (see page 31).

Native to: Eastern China.

Indocalamus tessellatus

Hardy, distinctive bamboo, also known as *Arundinaria ragamowskii*, *Sasa tessellata* and *Sasamorpha tessellata*, with slender, 1–1.5 m (3½–5 ft) long canes that often become splayed by the weight of foliage. However, it is ideal for creating a low screen or forming a focal point. The leaves are large, up to 60 cm (2 ft) long and 10 cm (4 in) wide, in warm and moist areas; in temperate and drier conditions, leaves 38 cm (15 in) long and 7.5 cm (3 in) wide are more common.

Some authorities claim that the leaves are the largest of any hardy bamboo.

Height: 1–1.5 m (3½–5 ft), sometimes more.

Spread/rootstock: Invasive, with spreading rhizomes.

Soil and situation: Fertile, moisture-retentive soil in light shade. It is ideal for creating attractive ground cover.

Propagation: Division of clumps and rhizome cuttings (see page 31).

Native to: Central China and Japan.

Phyllostachys aurea

Bamboo of Fairyland (UK) **Fishpole Bamboo** (UK/USA) **Golden Bamboo** (UK/USA)

Also known as *Bambusa aurea*, *Phyllostachys bambusoides* var. *aurea* and *Sinarundinaria aurea*, this hardy, graceful bamboo has bright green canes that mature to dull yellow when in full sun. The canes grow 3–4.5 m (10–15 ft) high and are 36 mm (1½ in) wide. The bright pea-green leaves are up to 15 cm (5 in) long and 18 mm (¾ in) wide. The young shoots are edible in spring.

Height: 3–3.6 m (10–12 ft), sometimes more.

Spread/rootstock: Moderately invasive, but easily checked.

Soil and situation: Fertile, moisture-retentive soil in full sun. It is superb when planted in tubs or large pots and positioned on a patio. It can also be used to form a hedge or screen.

Propagation: Division of clumps and cane offsets (see page 31).

Native to: Southeast China.

Native names: Gosan-chiku, Hotei-chiku, Kasan-chiku, Taibo-chiku.

COLOURFUL VARIETIES

There are several superb forms of *Phyllostachys aurea*, some with beautifully coloured canes and others with handsome leaves. Here are a few of them: • 'Albovariegata' – deep green, slender canes and mid-green leaves striped white. The white is most dominant in young leaves. • 'Flavescens Inversa' – thick, green canes with the grooved spaces around the leaf-joints becoming yellow. • 'Holochrysa' – thick, yellow canes, sometimes striped green. • 'Koi' – thick, green canes that become golden-yellow. • 'Variegata' – deep green canes; leaves with white stripes when young.

Phyllostachys aureosulcata aureocaulis

Forage Bamboo (USA)
Stake Bamboo (USA)
Yellow-groove Bamboo (UK/USA)

Vigorous, hardy, tall bamboo, also known as *Phyllostachys aureocaulis*, with canes 6 m (20 ft) or more high and 36 mm (1½ in) thick. They are golden-yellow, with greenish-yellow grooves. The shiny, mid-green leaves are up to 15 cm (6 in) long and 2.5 cm (1 in) wide. Related bamboos include 'Spectabilis' with golden-yellow canes, 'Harbin Inversa' with mainly yellow canes and a few green stripes, and 'Lama Temple' with richly yellow canes and fine, random stripes.

Height: 4.5–6 m (15–20 ft), sometimes more.

Spread/rootstock: Moderately invasive, but easily checked.

Soil and situation: Fertile, moisture-retentive soil in full sun.

Propagation: Division of clumps and cane offsets (see page 31).

Native to: Northeast China.

Phyllostachys bambusoides

Giant Timber Bamboo (UK/USA)

Also known as *Phyllostachys quilloi* and *Phyllostachys reticulata*, this large, dominant, hardy bamboo develops glossy green canes up to 6 m (20 ft) high. In its native area, canes in excess of 15 m (50 ft) are known. The leaves, about 18 cm (7 in) long and 36 mm (1½ in) wide, are dark green on the upper surface and sea-green below. Some leaves also have brown spots.

Height: Up to 6 m (20 ft), sometimes more.

Spread/rootstock: Moderately invasive, but easily checked.

Soil and situation: Fertile, moisture-retentive soil in full sun.

Propagation: Division of clumps and cane offsets (see page 31).

Native to: China.

Native names: Karadake, Ku-chiku, Mandake.

RECORD-BREAKING BAMBOO

The speed of growth of some bamboos is impressive and in Kyoto, Japan, a cane of *Phyllostachys bambusoides* is recorded as having grown about 1.2 m (4 ft) in 24 hours.

Phyllostachys bambusoides 'Castilloni'

Golden Brilliant Bamboo (UK/USA)

Also known as *Bambusa castillonis* and *Phyllostachys castillonis*, this hardy, graceful and exceptionally attractive bamboo has rich green canes with golden-yellow grooves. The bright green leaves are 7.5–15 cm (3–6 in) long and about 12 mm (½ in) wide.

Height: 2.4–4.5 m (8–15 ft), often more.

Spread/rootstock: Moderately invasive, but easily checked.

Soil and situation: Fertile, moisture-retentive soil in full sun.

Propagation: Division of clumps and cane offsets (see page 31).

Native to: China.

Native names: Hyondake, Ki mmei-chiku, Shimadake.

COLOURFUL VARIETIES

There are several other forms of *Phyllostachys bambusoides*, some with beautifully coloured canes. Here are a few of them:
• 'Castilloni Inversa' – thick, green canes, with yellow internodal grooves. • 'Castilloni Inversa Variegata' – thick, green canes with deep yellow, internodal grooves. The leaves are also attractive, being striped white and orange-tinted when young.
• 'Castilloni Variegata' – thick, golden-yellow canes with green, internodal grooves. Additionally, the green leaves are striped white. • 'Holochrysa' (also known as 'Allgold') – thick, golden-yellow canes that appear almost orange-yellow when seen in strong sunlight. • 'Kawadana' – thick, green canes with random splashes of yellow, which fade with age.

Phyllostachys edulis

Edible Bamboo (UK/USA) **Moso Bamboo** (USA)

Also known as *Phyllostachys heterocycla*, *Phyllostachys mitis* and *Phyllostachys pubescens*, this is the main source of young, edible bamboo shoots. The canes vary in size; in cooler areas canes up to 4.5 m (15 ft) and 36 mm (1½ in) are normal, but in many districts of China and Japan, as well as in southeast coastal areas of the USA, heights of 15 m (50 ft) or more have been recorded. The leaves are small and light to mid-green in colour.

Height: Depends on the area (see above).

Spread/rootstock: Invasive, but easily checked.

Soil and situation: Fertile, moisture-retentive soil in full sun.

Propagation: Division of clumps and cane offsets (see page 31).

Native to: China, Japan.

Native names: Mousou-chiku, Mosadake.

EDIBLE BAMBOO SHOOTS

It is the tender shoots that are eaten. They are left, when they emerge from the soil, until 15–30 cm (6–12 in) high. They are then cut, peeled and prepared in various ways, and are said to taste of celery or of a fusion of asparagus tips and oriental food. Usually, the flavour of the shoots depends on the sauce used with them.

Phyllostachys nigra

Black Bamboo (UK/USA) **Black-stemmed Bamboo** (UK/USA)

Also known as *Bambusa nigra*, *Phyllostachys puberula* var. *nigra* and *Sinarundinaria nigra*, this hardy, graceful, clump-forming bamboo has attractive canes, green at first but jet black within 2–3 years. Eventually, the canes grow up to 10.5 m (35 ft) or more high and 18–42 mm (¾–1¾ in) or more wide. However, in cool, temperate regions they tend to be shorter and more slender. The dark green leaves are up to 13 cm (5 in) long and 12 mm (½ in) wide.

Height: 2.4–3 m (8–10 ft), sometimes more.

Spread/rootstock: Moderately invasive, but easily checked.

Soil and situation: Fertile, moisture-retentive soil in full sun. However, the stems assume their best colours in dry soil. It is a versatile bamboo, and as well as being planted in a border can be put into a container on a patio or planted to form a hedge or screen.

Propagation: Division of clumps and cane offsets (see page 31).

Native to: Eastern and central China.

Native names: Kuro-chiku, Kurokake, Shiro-chiku.

COLOURFUL CONSIDERATIONS

There are several superb forms of *Phyllostachys nigra*. Here are a few of them: • 'Boryana' – thick, green canes, becoming brown and glossy. The whole plant has an attractive arching habit. • *henonis* – thick, bright green, upright canes and glossy green leaves. • 'Megurochiku' – thick, green canes that later develop black, internodal grooves. It is a distinctive bamboo, with an elegant appearance. • *punctata* – thick, green canes that slowly become almost black.

Phyllostachys vivax

Attractive and distinctive vigorous bamboo, with thick canes – said to have the largest diameter of any grown in Europe. In North America it has been recorded as growing more than 12 m (40 ft) high, with canes about 8 cm (3½ in) wide. Apart from the impressive size of the canes, it is best grown in the form *Phyllostachys vivax aureocaulis*, which has thick, rich yellow canes randomly striped green.

Height: 3–4.5 m (10–15 ft), sometimes more.

Spread/rootstock: Moderately invasive, but can be checked.

Soil and situation: Fertile, moisture-retentive soil in full sun.

Propagation: Division of clumps and cane offsets (see page 31).

Native to: Eastern China.

Pleioblastus chino

Hardy bamboo, also known as *Arundinaria chino* and *Bambusa chino*, with a somewhat scruffy and lax habit; nonetheless widely grown in its many forms thanks to their attractive leaves. Varieties include *aureostriatus* (light green leaves striped creamy-white) and *elegantissimus* (long and narrow leaves with thin white stripes). The species has dark green canes, usually blotched and stained with purplish markings, up to 2.1 m (7 ft) high and 12–18 mm (½–¾ in) wide.

Height: 1.5–2.1 m (5–7 ft).

Spread/rootstock: Invasive and spreading.

Soil and situation: Fertile, moisture-retentive soil in dappled sunlight. It is ideal for creating hedging and screening.

Propagation: Division of clumps and rhizome cuttings (see page 31).

Native to: Japan.

Native names: Azuma-nezasa, Shinegawadake.

Pleioblastus humilis var. *pumilis*

Also known as *Pleoblastus pumilus* and often now sold as *Pleioblastus argenteostriatus pumilus*, this hardy, dwarf bamboo has slender canes, green at first and later flushed purple. The dark green leaves remain attractive through the year.

Height: 1–1.5 m (3½–5 ft), sometimes slightly more.

Spread/rootstock: Invasive and spreading.

Soil and situation: Fertile, moisture-retentive soil in dappled sunlight. It can be planted to form attractive ground cover.

Propagation: Division of clumps and rhizome cuttings (see page 31).

Native to: Japan.

Pleioblastus pygmaeus

Dwarf Fern-leaf Bamboo (UK/USA)

Also known as *Arundinaria pygmaea*, *Bambusa pygmaea* and *Sasa pygmaea*, this hardy bamboo has slender canes, up to 20 cm (8 in) long, a neat, dwarf habit and brilliant green leaves.

Height: 30–45 cm (12–18 in).

Spread/rootstock: Invasive and spreading.

Soil and situation; Fertile, moisture-retentive but well-drained soil in good sunlight. It can be planted in containers on a patio, or used as a ground-cover plant.

Propagation: Division of clumps and rhizome cuttings (see page 31).

Native to: Japan (not known in the wild, but widely cultivated there).

Native names: Ke-oroshima-chiku, Ke-nezasa.

Pleioblastus simonii

Simon Bamboo (UK/USA)

Also known as *Arundinaria simonii*, *Bambusa simonii*, *Bambusa viridistriata* and *Nippocalamus simonii*, this hardy, vigorous bamboo has erect, olive-green canes that age to a dull green. They are up to 5.4 m (18 ft) high and 36 mm (1½ in) wide. The pale green leaves are up to 30 cm (1 ft) long on old and well-established canes, but smaller on young ones.

Height: 3.6–5.4 m (12–18 ft).

Spread/rootstock: Invasive and spreading.

Soil and situation: Fertile, moisture-retentive soil in light or dappled sunlight. It can be planted to form a hedge.

Propagation: Division of clumps and cane offsets (see page 31).

Native to: China and Japan.

Native names: Medake, Kawa-take.

Pleioblastus variegatus

Dwarf White-striped Bamboo (UK/USA)

Also known as *Arundinaria fortunei*, *Arundinaria variegata* and *Bambusa fortunei variegata*, this is one of the best white-variegated bamboos. However, although hardy it may lose some of its white-streaked leaves during severe winters. It has a dwarf nature, with pale green canes and leaves up to 20 cm (8 in) long and 2.5 cm (1 in) wide. The upper surface is dark green and striped white, fading to paler green.

Height: 30–75 cm (1–2½ ft).

Spread/rootstock: Invasive and spreading.

Soil and situation: Fertile, moisture-retentive soil in light shade. It is ideal for planting in a tub or large pot on a patio, as well as for attractive ground cover.

Propagation: Division of clumps and rhizome cuttings (see page 31).

Native to: Japan.

Native name: Chigo-zasa.

Pleioblastus viridistriatus

Golden-haired Bamboo (UK/USA)

Often known as *Arundinaria auricoma*, *Arundinaria viridistriata* and *Pleioblastus auricomus*, this is a superb hardy, miniature bamboo with slender, purple-green stems and brilliant golden-yellow variegated leaves, 20 cm (8 in) long and 42 mm (1¾ in) wide, with pea-green stripes. The cultivar 'Chrysophyllus' (sometimes listed as *chrysophylla*) has slender, purple-green canes and soft, golden-yellow leaves. It is best grown in partial shade as strong sun may cause scorching of the leaves. 'Bracken Hill' develops slender, purple-green canes and brilliant golden-yellow leaves striped green. Plant it in full sun.

Height: 90 cm–1.2 m (3–4 ft).

Spread/rootstock: Moderately invasive, but can be checked.

Soil and situation: Fertile, moisture-retentive soil in good light; this is especially important with this species for the production of colourful leaves. It is often planted in a container on a patio.

Propagation: Division of clumps (see page 31).

Native to: Japan.

Native name: Kamuro-zasa.

Pseudosasa amabilis

Tonkin Bamboo (UK/USA) **Tonkin Cane** (UK) **Tsingli Cane** (USA)

Also known as *Arundinaria amabilis*, this beautiful, moderately cold-resistant bamboo has tough, mid-green, thick-walled but pliable canes that arch at their tops. The canes vary in height, from 4.5 to 6 m (15–20 ft). The bright green leaves also range in length, from 10 to 30 cm (4–12 in) and up to 36 mm (1½ in) wide.

Height: 4.5–6 m (15–20 ft), sometimes more.

Spread: Moderately invasive, but easily checked.

Soil and situation: Fertile, moisture-retentive but well-drained soil in full sun or light shade. Unfortunately, it is not suitable for cold areas. It is often used to create screens and hedges.

Propagation: Division of clumps and cane offsets (see page 31).

Native to: Southern China.

SOURCE OF GARDEN CANES

Most garden canes imported from East Asia to Europe are *Pseudosasa amabilis*. At one time, the majority of fishing rods were made from it, while large canes were used for pole vaulting. Canes were also once used as ski sticks.

Pseudosasa japonica

Arrow Bamboo (UK/USA) **Metake** (UK/USA)

Also known as *Arundinaria japonica*, *Bambusa japonica*, *Bambusa metake* and *Sasa japonica*, this hardy bamboo has sharply pointed, oblong to lance-shaped, dark glossy green leaves, about 23 cm (10 in) long and 30 mm (1¼ in) wide. It forms a large, tall thicket, often 4.5 m (15 ft) high, and is ideal for screening as well as forming a hedge.

Height: 2.4–4.5 m (8–15 ft).

Spread/rootstock: Moderately invasive, but easily checked.

Soil and situation: Fertile, moisture-retentive but well-drained soil in full sun or light shade. Unfortunately, it is not suitable for cold areas. It can, however, be used as a windbreak and for planting in a container on a patio.

Propagation: Division of clumps, cane offsets and rhizome cuttings (see page 31).

Native to: China, Japan and Korea.

Native names: Metake, Yadake.

COLOURFUL VARIATIONS

There are several superb forms of *Pseudosasa japonica*, some with beautifully coloured leaves. Here are two: • 'Akebono' – large leaves, yellowish-white at the tip and changing to yellowish-green at the base. It is best planted in a shaded position. • 'Akebonosuji' – attractive leaves, most striped creamy-white, with a few remaining plain green. However, some resemble the leaves seen in 'Akebono'.

Sasa palmata

Also known as *Arundinaria palmata*, *Bambusa metallica* and *Bambusa palmata*, this somewhat rampant bamboo is best reserved for planting where it can roam at will. The dull green canes, brilliant green when young, grow up to 2.4 m (8 ft) high and bear thick and leathery, bright green leaves, up to 35 cm (14 in) long and 8 cm (3½ in) wide. Unfortunately, in cold weather the tips and sides of the leaves often wither. However, this does not damage the rest of the bamboo and it invariably recovers during the following summer.

Height: 1.5–2.4m (5–8 ft).

Spread/rootstock: Extremely invasive.

Soil and situation: Fertile, moisture-retentive soil in dappled light. It is often used to create attractive ground cover.

Propagation: Division of clumps and rhizome cuttings (see page 31).

Native to: Japan.

Native name: Chimakizasa, Kumaizasa.

SOURCE OF PAPER

In East Asia, *Sasa palmata*, as well as a few other bamboos, has been used to produce paper pulp for the publishing industry. As far back as 1875, there were discussions about the use of crushed, young canes, with general interest for this coming from England, India and America.

Sasa palmata nebulosa

Also known as *Sasa cernua* 'Nebulosa', it is similar to *Sasa palmata* but not as rampant. The canes often emerge in a long curve, and instead of being brilliant green assume purple-brown blotches. Also, the leaves are slightly larger, and a rich, glossy-green.

Height: 1.5–2.4 m (5–8 ft).

Spread/rootstock: Invasive nature.

Soil and situation: Fertile, moisture-retentive soil in dappled light. It is often planted to create ground cover.

Propagation: Division of clumps and rhizome cuttings (see page 31).

Native to: Japan.

Sasa veitchii

Kuma Bamboo Grass (USA)

Also known as *Arundinaria veitchii*, *Bambusa veitchii* and *Sasa albomarginata*, this hardy, invasive and low-growing bamboo has slender, purple-green canes, up to 1.5 cm (5 ft) high and 2.5 cm (1 in) wide. The glossy, smooth-surfaced, deep and rich green leaves, up to 25 cm (10 in) long and about 6 cm (2½ in) wide, have withered edges and tips during winter that create an attractive papery look.

Height: 90 cm–1.5 m (3–5 ft).

Spread/rootstock: Spreading and invasive.

Soil and situation: Fertile, moisture-retentive soil in dappled light. It is often planted as ground cover.

Propagation: Division of clumps and rhizome cuttings (see page 31).

Native to: Japan.

Native name: Kumazasa.

Sasaella masamuneana 'Albostriata'

Hardy bamboo with slender canes, up to 1.2 m (4 ft) high, and medium to large leaves, 18 cm (7 in) long and 5 cm (2 in) wide, which have white stripes when young. Unfortunately, by autumn the attractive markings are less noticeable and during winter they often disappear. However, it is an ideal bamboo for creating attractive ground cover during summer.

Height: 90 cm–1.2 m (3–4 ft).

Spread/rootstock: Invasive.

Soil and situation: Fertile, moisture-retentive soil in dappled light.

Propagation: Division of clumps and rhizome cuttings (see page 31).

Native to: Japan.

Sasaella ramosa

Dwarf Bamboo (UK/USA)

Also known as *Arundinaria ramosa*, *Arundinaria vagans*, *Bambusa ramosa* and *Sasa ramosa*, this hardy, easily grown and exceedingly rampant and vigorous ground-covering bamboo has bright green canes, up to 1.5 m (5 ft) high, that mature to deep olive. The mid-green leaves, dull greyish-green beneath, are about 15 cm (6 in) long and 18 mm (¾ in) wide. It is ideal for covering banks and large areas. However, it is invasive and should be planted only where it can spread freely.

Height: 90 cm–1.5 m (3–5 ft).

Spread/rootstock: Spreading and invasive.

Soil and situation: Fertile, moisture-retentive soil in dappled light. It is often planted to create attractive ground cover.

Propagation: Division of clumps and rhizome cuttings (see page 31).

Native to: Japan.

Native name: Azuma-zasa.

Semiarundinaria fastuosa

Narihira Bamboo (USA)

Also known as *Arundinaria fastuosa*, *Arundinaria narihira*, *Bambusa fastuosa* and *Phyllostachys fastuosa*, this hardy, popular bamboo has deep glossy green canes, tinged purple when young and maturing to purple-brown, especially when in good light. The ramrod-straight canes are up to 7.5 m (25 ft) tall and often 42 mm (1¾ in) wide. The leaves, up to 25 cm (10 in) long and 2.5 cm (1 in) wide, are brilliant green on the upper surface, but duller and greyish-green beneath. The form *viridis* is also attractive, with thick, rich green canes that mature to yellowish-green. Additionally, the leaves are rich green. It usually grows taller than the species.

Height: 7.5 m (25 ft).

Spread/rootstock: Moderately invasive, but easily checked.

Soil and situation: Fertile, moisture-retentive soil in full sun or shade. It is a versatile bamboo and when young can be planted in containers on a patio, as well as being used as a windbreak.

Propagation: Division of clumps, cane offsets and rhizome cuttings (see page 31).

Native to: Southern Japan.

Native name: Narihadake.

Semiarundinaria yashadake kimmei

Hardy and distinctive bamboo with thick, fairly straight, rich golden-yellow canes, often 5.4 m (18 ft) or more high, and small, dark green leaves. It is ideal for creating colour and is claimed to be equal to any colour-stemmed *Phyllostachys*.

Height: 3.6–5.4 m (12–18 ft), sometimes more.

Spread/rootstock: Moderately invasive, but easily checked.

Soil and situation: Fertile, moisture-retentive soil in full sun or shade. Often, it is planted in a tub or a large pot on a patio.

Propagation: Division of clumps, cane offsets and rhizome cuttings (see page 31).

Native to: Japan.

Shibataea kumasaca

Also known as *Bambusa kumasaca, Phyllostachys kumasasa, Phyllostachys ruscifolia* and *Sasa ruscifolia*, this hardy, distinctive bamboo has triangular to slightly elliptical dull brown canes, 1.5–1.8 m (5–6 ft) high, which are pale green when young. The 10 cm (4 in) long and 2.5 cm (1 in) wide leaves are dark green at first but quickly change to dull yellowish-green. It tends to form a clump and in cooler areas is usually seen no higher than 90 cm (3 ft). Some authorities suggest that a clump of this bamboo resembles the growth habit of *Ruscus aculeatus* (Butcher's Broom, Box Holly or Jew's Myrtle).

The form *aureostriata* has broader leaves, striped creamy-yellow. However, the variegations are not reliable and sometimes entire leaves become yellow.

Height: 90 cm (3 ft), sometimes more, occasionally up to 1.8 m (6 ft).

Spread/rootstock: Moderately invasive, but easily checked.

Soil and situation: Fertile, moisture-retentive soil and light shade. It is often used as ground cover, and is ideal for planting in a tub or a large pot on a patio.

Propagation: Division of clumps and rhizome cuttings (see page 31).

Native to: China and Japan.

Native names: Bundodake, Bungozasa, Gomaizasa, Kagurasasa, Lyozasa, Okamesaza.

Thamnocalamus crassinodus

Also known as *Fargesia crassinoda*, this hardy bamboo has canes initially with a grey bloom but later becoming yellow-green. They are usually 3–4.5 m (10–15 ft) high, although in warm and moist areas they are recorded as 7.5 m (25 ft) high. When exposed to strong sunlight they assume a red tint. There is also a distinctive swelling above the leaf-joints on the canes. It is not hardy in cold areas, especially when exposed to cold, harsh winds.

Height: 3–4.5 m (10–15 ft), or more.

Spread/rootstock: Clump-forming and non-invasive.

Soil and situation: Fertile, moisture-retentive soil in full sun. When planted in good light, the canes are more attractive. It is often planted in a tub or a large pot on a patio.

Propagation: Division of clumps and cane offsets (see page 31).

Native to: Tibet.

FOR EXTRA COLOUR

There are three superb forms of *Thamnocalamus crassinodus*, each slightly hardier than the species: • 'Kew Beauty' – the canes develop reddish shades, especially when in strong sunlight; small leaves. • 'Lang Tang' (sometimes written as 'Langtang') – the canes become yellowish-green when exposed to strong sunlight; small leaves. • 'Merlyn' – the canes become yellowish-green when exposed to strong sunlight; small leaves.

Thamnocalamus spathiflorus

Also known as *Arundinaria spathiflora*, this hardy, elegant and handsome bamboo has canes up to 4.5 m (15 ft) high and 2.5 cm (1 in) wide. Throughout their first season they have a grey, bluish-white bloom. Later they are bright green, maturing to pinkish-purple when exposed to sunlight. The 13–15 cm (5–6 in) long and 12 mm (½ in) wide leaves are pale, soft green.

Height: 4.5 m (15 ft), sometimes more.

Spread/rootstock: Clump-forming and non-invasive.

Soil and situation: Fertile, moisture-retentive soil. It is best in light shade and shelter from strong, cold wind. It can be planted in a tub or a large pot and positioned on a patio.

Propagation: Division of clumps and cane offsets (see page 31).

Native to: Northwest Himalayas.

WALKING STICKS AND UMBRELLA HANDLES

Thamnocalamus spathiflorus is grown in India, and at one time provided most of the material used in the manufacture of walking sticks, pipe stems and umbrella handles.

Thamnocalamus tessellatus

Also known as *Arundinaria tessellata*, this hardy bamboo is the only species native to South Africa. The canes, up to 3.6 m (12 ft) high or more and 12 mm (½ in) thick, are upright in habit, pale green at first, maturing to deep green and eventually changing to dull purple. This purple is best seen when the bamboo is grown in an exposed position. The mid-green, 5–13 cm (2–5 in) long leaves are mid- to dark green.

Height: 2.4–3.6 m (8–12 ft), sometimes more.

Spread/rootstock: Clump-forming and non-invasive.

Soil and situation: Fertile, moisture-retentive soil and light shade. It grows best when sheltered from cold, strong wind. It can be planted in a container on a patio, and can also be used to form a hedge.

Propagation: Division of clumps and rhizome cuttings (see page 31).

Native to: South Africa.

Native name: Bergbamboes.

Yushania anceps

Also known as *Arundinaria anceps*, *Chimonobambusa jaunsarensis* and *Sinoarundinaria anceps*, this vigorous, clump-forming bamboo has straight, erect, at first deep, glossy green canes, later dull green-brown. Usually they are up to 3.6 m (12 ft) high. The leaves are mid-green and up to 15 cm (6 in) long and 12 mm (½ in) wide. It is ideal as a screen or hedge. It is not hardy in cold and exposed areas.

Height: 3–3.6 m (10–12 ft), sometimes more.

Spread/rootstock: Spreading and invasive.

Soil and situation: Fertile, moisture-retentive but well-drained soil in full sun or light shade. It is not suitable for very cold areas, but in milder places is ideal for forming a screen.

Propagation: Division of clumps and cane offsets (see page 31).

Native to: Central and northwest Himalayas.

Yushania anceps 'Pitt White'

This distinctive bamboo, a clone of *Yushania anceps* and also known as *Arundinaria niitikayamensis* (Pitt White Clone), is a distinctive and exceptionally vigorous bamboo. Although it is slightly tender, its speed of growth has been recorded at 15 cm (6 in) within a period of 24 hours, producing canes more than 9 m (30 ft) high and up to 36 mm (1½ in) thick. The rich green, glossy leaves are about 7.5 cm (3 in) long and 12 mm (½ in) wide.

Height: to 9 m (30 ft).

Spread/rootstock: Spreading and very invasive.

Soil and situation: Fertile, moisture-retentive but well-drained soil in full sun or light shade. It is not suitable for very cold areas.

Propagation: Division of clumps and cane offsets (see page 31).

WAR EVACUEE

This clone is far more vigorous than the species and was originally taken in about 1940 from Perry's Hardy Plant Farm in North London to the Pitt White Garden, Uplyme, East Devon, England. Stocks of this bamboo were obliterated a year or so later when Perry's Hardy Plant Farm gave its full attention to growing food during the second world war. Later, propagation material from this clone was distributed around the world from Pitt White garden.

FURTHER BAMBOOS TO CONSIDER

The range of bamboos is wide. As well as the ones that have been described and illustrated in the A–Z of bamboos, here are others to consider.

- *Drepanostachyum microphyllum* Slightly tender bamboo with glossy, dark green canes that mature to purple. It is clump-forming and non-invasive, with canes about 3.6 m (12 ft) high.

- *Himalayacalamus hookerianus* Popularly known as the Blue Bamboo and also as *Drepanostachyum hookerianum*, this slightly tender bamboo has yellow canes with many green stripes. In sunlight they assume shades of red and pink. It is clump-forming and non-invasive, with canes to about 7.5 m (25 ft) high.

- *Indocalamus longiauritus* Moderately hardy bamboo, similar to *Indocalamus latifolius* (see page 40) but with narrower and more pointed leaves. It is moderately invasive and can grow 1.5–2.1 m (5–7 ft) high, although usually less.

- *Indocalamus tesselatus hamadae* Also known as *Indocalamus hamadae,* its long and broad leaves are claimed to be the largest of any cultivated temperate bamboo, up to 60 cm (2 ft) long. It is invasive, with canes up to 4.5 m (15 ft) high.

- *Phyllostachys arcana* **'Luteosulcata'** Attractive bamboo, with thick, green canes with yellow grooves between the joints; lower ones have a zigzag appearance. It is moderately invasive, with canes about 6 m (20 ft) high, sometimes more.

- *Phyllostachys propinqua* **'Bicolor'** Distinctive bamboo, with thick, soft-yellow canes with green stripes. It is moderately invasive, with canes about 6 m (20 ft) high, sometimes more.

- *Phyllostachys rubromarginata* Attractive canes, thick, glaucous green and maturing to grey or yellowish-grey. It is moderately invasive, with canes growing up to 9 m (30 ft) high.

- *Pseudosasa japonica* **var.** *pleioblastoides* Also known as *Pseudosasa pleioblastoides*, this handsome and wind-tolerant bamboo has green canes. It is moderately invasive, with canes growing up to 3.6 m (12 ft) high, sometimes slightly more.

- *Sasa kurilensis* **(dwarf form)** Hardy, slender and dwarf bamboo, with green canes up to 1.2 m (4 ft) high and 12 mm (½ in) thick. The large, dark, glossy-green leaves are up to 20 cm (8 in) long and 12–18 mm (½–¾ in) wide; during cold winters and dry periods, they sometimes wither along their edges. Nevertheless, it is a handsome bamboo, but invasive.

- *Sasa tsuboiana* Beautiful hardy bamboo with slender, upright canes, growing up to 1.5 m (5 ft) high, and with large leaves, up to 25 cm (10 in) long and 5 cm (2 in) wide, that can sometimes become withered along their edges during spells of cold weather. It is moderately invasive, but easily checked.

- *Semiarundinaria kagamiana* Vigorous, with deep green canes that with maturity assume crimson shades when in good light. It is moderately vigorous, with canes growing to about 6 m (30 ft) high.

- *Semiarundinaria yamadorii* The green canes mature to an attractive yellow-green, with mid- to yellow leaves. It is a moderately vigorous bamboo, with canes growing to about 6 m (20 ft) high.

- *Yushania maculata* Beautiful bamboo, with blue-grey new canes, maturing to olive-green. It is invasive and vigorous, with canes about 3 m (10 ft) high, sometimes slightly more.

- *Yushania maling* Greyish-green canes, becoming brownish-green, with a rough surface. It is vigorous and invasive, with canes about 3 m (10 ft) high.

BAMBOOS FOR CONSERVATORIES

Several bamboos are too tender to be grown outdoors in temperate climates and therefore are best reserved for planting in a tub or a large pot in a warm conservatory. As well as warmth, they require positions with plenty of light. Here are two to consider:

- *Bambusa multiplex* **'Floribunda'** Also known as *Bambusa multiplex* 'Fernleaf', this non-invasive and clump-forming bamboo has slender, dull green canes that mature to dull yellow. However, it is the small, plain green leaves, borne in fern-like clusters, that first catch the eye. It usually grows to a height of 1.5–2.4 m (5–8 ft) in a container, but plants up to 5.4 m (18 ft) tall have been reported in warm areas.

- *Bambusa ventricosa* Known as 'Buddha's Belly', this distinctive, tender bamboo, which is usually imported into temperate countries, has thick, dark green canes that are swollen between their joints. These are especially noticeable when the plant is constricted in a small pot. It usually grows to 1.5 m (5 ft) high in a container, but can grow up to 2.4 m (8 ft) in warm areas.

Grasses and sedges to consider

Are they difficult to grow?

Ornamental grasses are easy to grow, whether they are annual, herbaceous or shrubby and long-lasting like *Cortaderia selloana*, the well-known Pampas Grass. Unlike some bamboos, ornamental grasses are not invasive and even the tall and majestic *Miscanthus sacchariflorus*, which can be used to create a dominant screen up to 3 m (10 ft) high, is not a problem. Grasses and sedges can bring a striking new element to your garden in return for very little work.

WHAT ARE GRASSES AND SEDGES?

Grasses belong to the Poaceae, one of the largest plant families, and include food plants such as maize, wheat, rye, oats and barley. Some grasses are purely ornamental, while others are useful lawn and meadow species.

Sedges belong to the Cyperaceae family and include the genus *Carex*. In general, they are evergreen plants, even when growing in cold areas. They have rhizomatous roots and some have saw-like edges to their leaves. Their stems are usually triangular or solid, making them stiffer plants than grasses. This helps to produce an upright or semi-cascading habit.

Holcus mollis *'Albovariegatus' is a hardy perennial grass with variegated leaves.*

Above: Cortaderia selloana (*Pampas Grass), with its large, plume-like flowerheads, creates a dramatic feature, either in a border formed of a medley of herbaceous perennials and shrubs, or in a large bed in a lawn.*

The many variegated forms of Hakonechloa macra *form attractive features in borders and, especially, at the edges of raised beds.*

ANNUAL ORNAMENTAL GRASSES

There are many easily grown annual grasses that can be used to decorate borders, perhaps filling gaps between other plants in herbaceous and mixed borders. They can be raised by sowing seeds (see page 60). Some of these grasses, including *Anthoxanthum gracile*, which has a fresh coumarin fragrance when the leaves are bruised, are superb when cut and dried for use in flower arrangements indoors during winter.

Hardy annual grasses
- *Agrostis nebulosa* (Cloud Grass) – see page 62.
- *Anthoxanthum gracile* (Annual Vernal Grass) – see page 71.
- *Avena sterilis* (Animated Oat) – see page 63.
- *Briza maxima* (Great Quaking Grass, Pearl Grass and Puffed Wheat) – see page 64.
- *Bromus briziformis* (Brome and Rattlesnake Chess) – see page 64.
- *Hordeum jubatum* (Fox-tail Barley, Squirrel-tail Barley and Squirrel-tail Grass) – see page 68.
- *Sporobolus pulchellus* (also known as *Agrostis pulchella* and commonly as Dropseed and Rush Grass) – see page 71.

Half-hardy ornamental grass
- *Coix lacryma-jobi* (Christ's Tears and Job's Tears) – see page 66.

GRASS BORDERS

Borders and beds formed of ornamental grasses have become immensely popular; they are interesting to the eye and fascinating to the ear. Even the gentlest breeze makes their tops dance and rustle, introducing further interesting qualities into a garden.

Herbaceous ornamental grasses create the most dominant features, and once planted can be left alone until they are congested and their quality diminishes. Congested clumps can be lifted and divided (see page 61).

Where there is a small bed, or perhaps a wind-sheltered corner, you could consider a planting solely of *Miscanthus sinensis* and its many varieties. There is a wide range of these, in different heights and colours (several are described on page 68).

As well as creating dedicated grass borders, tall species form backgrounds for herbaceous plants or help to partition large gardens into smaller and more manageable parts.

Several forms of Miscanthus sinensis *have a ground-covering habit. There are many to choose from, including both low-growing and variegated types.*

ENCOURAGING BIRDS

Grasses often encourage birds into gardens. However, remember that garden birds will not venture into dense undergrowth created by tall grasses, and they mainly eat seeds after they have fallen to the ground. Birds with these eating habits include finches and sparrows.

Sedges to consider

There are several species of Carex *that will brighten gardens and containers, including:*

- *Carex elata* 'Aurea' (also known as *Carex elata* 'Bowles' Golden') – see page 65.
- *Carex oshimensis* 'Evergold' (also known as *Carex morrowii* 'Evergold') – see page 65.
- *Carex phyllocephala* 'Sparkler' (also known as *Carex phyllocephala* 'Fuiri Tenjiku-suge') – see page 65.
- *Carex pilulifera* 'Tinney's Princess' – see page 71.

Carex testacea *has narrow, pale olive leaves (see page 66)*

Grasses in containers

Many grasses are ideal for planting in containers and some have a cascading habit that cloaks the container's upper edges. Regular watering is essential, from spring to autumn, to ensure that the compost does not become dry. One practical bonus is that grasses in containers are less vulnerable to the ravages of snails and slugs than plants in borders. Even where these pests are a nuisance, they can be deterred by encircling the containers with slippery tapes.

GRASSES AND SEDGES FOR CONTAINERS

When you are selecting grasses, choose containers that harmonize with the plants. For example, *Festuca glauca* has a tufted and spiky appearance that is ideal for containers with ornate sides. In contrast, *Hakonechloa macra* 'Alboaurea' is cascading, and is best planted in a small tub, where it masks the container's edges.

There are many grasses suitable for growing in containers, including:

- *Acorus gramineus* 'Ogon' – initially upright, then arching. This attractive grass has narrow and tapering green leaves with golden variegated bands right along their lengths (see page 62).
- *Carex oshimensis* 'Evergold' – arching. It has stiff, arching leaves variegated green and yellow. There are other *Carex* species suitable for containers (see page 65).
- *Festuca glauca* – tufted. There are several varieties, some dwarf but most with coloured leaves, including blue, blue-green and silvery-blue (see page 67).
- *Hakonechloa macra* 'Alboaurea' – cascading. It has long and narrow leaves striped gold and off-white (see page 67).

IDEAS FOR PLANTING IN CONTAINERS

Steps

↗ *Cascading herbaceous grasses in containers are ideal for decorating the tops of wide steps*

Winter display

↗ *A medley of Carex spp. and narrow-leaved border plants creates a fine display*

Window box

↗ *Windowboxes are enhanced by symmetrical arrangements of coloured-leaved grasses*

Roof garden

↗ *Small pots of low-growing grasses are ideal for decorating windswept roof gardens*

Decking

↗ *For a dramatic feature, colour harmonize the foliage of grasses with the container*

Pond

↗ *A medley of grasses and palms introduces a Mediterranean ambience to water features*

PLANTING AND LOOKING AFTER GRASSES IN CONTAINERS

Thorough preparation of a container and the use of pest- and disease-free compost are essential. Here are the steps to success:

1 Check that the container is clean and free from old compost, which might harbour pests and diseases. Thoroughly wash and scrub both the inside and outside, rinse in clean water and allow to dry.

2 If it is large, place the container in its display position. Stand tubs on three bricks to reduce the risk of slugs and snails reaching the plants. Check that drainage holes in the container's base are not blocked.

3 Place broken clay pots or clean drainage material over the drainage holes. Add a 12–18 mm (½–¾ in) thick layer of coarse shingle. Half-fill the container with clean, loam-based potting compost. Gently firm it.

4 The day before planting a container-grown plant into a tub or large pot in a garden, thoroughly water the compost. It is essential that the compost is moist. If it is dry, the plant will not become established quickly.

5 Carefully remove the rootball from the container and position it in the centre of the tub or large pot. The surface of the rootball should be about 2.5 cm (1 in) below the rim of the tub or pot.

6 Some plants have a 'face' side, one that is more attractive than any other. Therefore, turn the plant until this faces the main viewing position. Then, add and firm further compost, so that its surface is about 2.5 cm (1 in) below the rim. Use a watering-can (with the rose turned upwards) to water the compost several times.

LOOKING AFTER GRASSES IN CONTAINERS

- Watering is the main task and must not be neglected. On warm days it may be necessary to water the compost several times, especially if the container is small. If the compost does become dry, thoroughly water it; wait until the compost swells and fills gaps between the compost and the inside of the tub or large pot, then again add water.

- Feeding is not necessary during the first year, but in late spring of the following year use a liquid fertilizer applied when watering. Try not to wet the foliage.

- Tidy up plants in late autumn or early spring by removing dead leaves.

- Slugs and snails can be deterred in several ways, apart from standing the container on three bricks. Broken eggshells deter them, while saucers of beer, water and sugar entice and trap them. Remove dead or intoxicated slugs every morning. However, ensure that hedgehogs cannot get at the mixture.

Tidying up grasses

Smarten up grasses growing in containers by using sharp scissors or secateurs to trim off old stems and leaves.

Raising and looking after ornamental grasses

Should I sow seeds or buy plants?

I t is best to buy healthy, established herbaceous grasses from garden centres or specialist nurseries. Hardy annual grasses can be raised from seeds sown in spring directly where they are to grow. Half-hardy annual grasses are best raised from seeds sown in early or mid-spring in gentle warmth. In later years, congested herbaceous plants can be lifted and divided in spring. Always wear gloves when handling the sharp leaves of *Cortaderia selloana* (Pampas Grass).

BUYING GRASSES

This is best done in spring, so that plants have until late summer to become established before the onset of cold weather. In theory, plants sold in containers can be planted at any time of the year when the weather and soil allow, but grasses are certainly at their brightest and most attractive in early and mid-summer and therefore are best planted in spring.

RAISING HARDY GRASSES

Use a rake to level the surface of the soil

Sow seeds in mid-spring, when all risk of severe frost has passed. If the soil was not prepared during the autumn or early winter of the previous year, lightly fork it over. Use the back of a garden fork to break down large clumps, then shuffle sideways over the area to firm the soil. Use a garden rake to level the surface.

Usually, only a small area is sown. Scatter a few seeds on the soil's surface and careful rake them into the top soil. Lightly water the surface, taking care not to scatter the seeds. Place a piece of fine-mesh wire-netting over the seeds to protect them from the ravages of birds and mice.

Alternatively, use the pointed end of a stick to form drills about 6 mm (¼ in) deep. Sow seeds thinly, then draw friable soil over them and lightly firm it. Gently water the soil.

Sow seeds thinly and evenly in shallow drills

Briza maxima (Great Quaking Grass) is a hardy annual grass with an upright growth habit and spectacular flowers formed of heart-shaped spikelets.

LOOKING AFTER GRASSES

- **Annual and half-hardy grasses:** In late autumn or early winter, pull up and discard plants. However, a few annual grasses are naturally herbaceous in mild areas and will produce fresh shoots during the following spring.
- **Herbaceous grasses:** With the onset of cold weather in the autumn or early winter, the foliage and stems will die back. In cold areas, the topgrowth can be left in position until the following spring to protect the plants. Elsewhere, pull or cut away all stems and leaves in autumn or early winter.
- **Perennial grasses:** In spring, cut or pull away dead leaves. The leaves may have sharp edges, so always wear strong gloves.

LIFTING AND DIVIDING HERBACEOUS GRASSES

In most temperate climates, lifting and dividing congested clumps of herbaceous grasses is best performed in spring.

1 *If shoots and stems from the previous year's growth are still on the plant, carefully pull or cut them off. Then use a garden fork to lift the entire plant from the ground. Place it on a piece of old sacking.*

2 *Use a couple of small garden forks to separate the clump into good-sized pieces. Discard the old, central part of the clump and use only young pieces from around the outside. Do not break the clump into very small pieces as they will not create a bold display during the same year.*

3 *If there will be a delay before you replant the young pieces of herbaceous grass, place them on a damp piece of hessian and cover them. Friable soil around clumps soon becomes dry and the roots rapidly suffer. If there will be a long delay before planting, lightly water the roots, as well as the hessian.*

4 *Prepare the planting site by removing all weeds, especially perennial types. Fork the soil and level the surface. If the soil is dry, lightly but thoroughly water it and leave until the following day before planting. Never put plants into dry soil.*

5 *Before planting, space out the plants on the soil's surface. To create dramatic features plant them in threes, forming a triangle. Use a trowel to dig a planting hole. Spread out the roots and position them slightly deeper than before. Then spread and firm the soil around them.*

6 *When planting is complete, level the soil with the prongs of a garden fork to remove depressions and bumps. Then, lightly but thoroughly water the soil and insert a label near to the plants. It is necessary to keep the soil moist to ensure that plants become rapidly established.*

TROUBLESHOOTING GRASS PROBLEMS

- Grasses are resilient plants, having fibrous root systems and leaves that tend to roll and conserve moisture in the plant when water is in short supply.
- Once established, grasses in borders are usually able to survive slight shortages of water, but be prepared to water them during a drought. Grasses in containers, however, will need regular watering. Narrow-leaved ornamental grasses survive dry soil better than those with wider leaves, although even these usually only sustain damage to their tips and edges.
- Grasses do not usually suffer from pests and diseases, although in wet seasons they may suffer from rust. Keeping a good circulation of air around plants and not making the foliage wet helps them to survive.
- Mealy bugs occasionally attack *Miscanthus* spp., infesting roots as well as leaves. Use a systemic insecticide.

A–Z of ornamental grasses and sedges

Are there many different types?

The range of ornamental grasses is wide, and includes those with variegated leaves that are ideal for planting in a container on a patio or in a raised bed, as well as others that create dense screens. There is also the dominant and widely planted *Cortaderia selloana* (**Pampas Grass**), which is often grown as a specimen plant in a circular bed in a lawn, and even the widely grown food plant, *Zea mays* (**Corn-on-the-Cob**), with many variegated forms (see page 71).

Acorus calamus 'Argenteostriatus'

Variegated Sweet Flag (UK/USA)

Also known as *Acorus calamus* 'Variegatus', this hardy perennial grass is ideal for planting at the edge of a garden pond or in a bog garden that does not dry out during summer. It develops long, erect, sword-like green leaves striped cream and yellow, and creates a dominant feature. When bruised, the roots and leaves are highly aromatic.

Height: 45–75 cm (18–30 in).

Spread: 45 cm (18 in), sometimes more.

Soil and situation: As a marginal plant at the edge of a garden pond, in 7.5 cm (3 in) of water, or in a bog garden.

Raising new plants: Lift and divide congested plants in spring (see page 61).

Acorus gramineus 'Ogon'

Variegated Grassy-leaved Sweet Flag (USA)

Superb, hardy, perennial grass, initially upright then arching, with narrow and tapering green leaves that have golden, variegated bands along their lengths. It is ideal for planting in a large pot or small tub on a patio. You could also try it in a raised bed. There are several other variegated forms, including 'Hakuro-nishiki' (variegated leaves), 'Variegatus' (also known as 'Aureovariegatus', with leaves striped cream and yellow) and 'Yodo-no-yuki' (leaves variegated pale green).

Height: 38–45 cm (15–18 in).

Spread: 38–50 cm (15–20 in).

Soil and situation: Moderately fertile, well-drained but moisture-retentive soil and full sun or light shade.

Raising new plants: Lift and divide congested plants in spring (see page 61).

Agrostis nebulosa

Cloud Grass (UK/USA)

Hardy annual grass with a slender, branching, often lax habit and flat, dark green leaves. It is ideal for drying and displaying in bouquets.

Height: 30 cm (1 ft).

Spread: 15–20 cm (6–8 in).

Soil and situation: Moderately fertile, light, well-drained soil in full sun or partial shade.

Raising new plants: Sow seeds in spring, each year (see page 60).

Alopecurus pratensis 'Aureovariegatus'

Variegated Meadow Foxtail (UK/USA)

Also known as *Alopecurus pratensis* 'Variegatus', it is a beautiful clump-forming perennial grass with narrow, green leaves boldly striped and edged in gold. There are other excellent forms, including 'Aureus', with all-gold leaves.

Height: 75–90 cm (2½–3 ft).

Spread: 75–90 cm (2½–3 ft).

Soil and situation: Moderately fertile, well-drained soil and full sun or light shade.

Raising new plants: Lift and divide congested plants in spring (see page 61).

Anthoxanthum odoratum

Sweet Vernal Grass (UK/USA)

Hardy perennial grass with clustered, slender, shiny, green leaf blades that become straw-coloured. The leaves are fragrant when bruised or cut and are sometimes used in garlands or dried flower displays.

Height: 45–50 cm (18–20 in).

Spread: 30–45 cm (12–18 in).

Soil and situation: Poor to moderately fertile, moisture-retentive but well-drained soil in full sun or partial shade.

Raising new plants: Lift and divide congested plants in spring (see page 61).

Arundo donax

Cana Brava (USA) **Carrizo** (USA)
Giant Reed (UK/USA) **Provence Reed** (USA)

Perennial, clump-forming and rhizomatous-rooted, somewhat bamboo-like grass with stems clothed in graceful and arching, lance-shaped, glaucous green leaves. During autumn it develops numerous spikelets, forming a large, compact head, 30–38 cm (12–15 in) long; first they are reddish, slowly becoming white.

Height: 1.8–3 m (6–10 ft).

Spread: 90 cm–1.5 m (3–5 ft).

Soil and situation: Light, well-drained but moisture-retentive in full sun and a wind-sheltered position.

Raising new plants: Lift and divide congested clumps in spring (see page 61).

Arundo donax var. versicolor

Variegated Giant Reed (UK/USA)

Also known as *Arundo donax* 'Variegata', this perennial, clump-forming, rhizomatous, somewhat bamboo-like grass has stems clothed in graceful and arching, lance-shaped, glaucous-green leaves striped and edged in dull white. There are other variegated forms, including 'Aureovariegata' and 'Golden Chain'. 'Macrophylla' has stems tinted mauve, and glaucous, grey-green leaves with shades of blue-green.

Height: 1.8–2.4 m (6–8 ft).

Spread: 90 cm–1.2 m (3–4 ft).

Soil and situation: Light, well-drained but moisture-retentive in full sun and a wind-sheltered position.

Raising new plants: Lift and divide congested clumps in spring (see page 61).

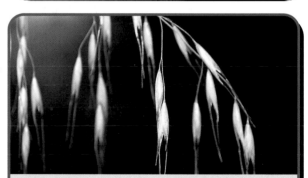

Avena sterilis

Animated Oat (UK/USA)

Hardy annual with an upright or slightly spreading habit and narrow leaves up to 30 cm (1 ft) long. The flowerheads and stems are sometimes used in dried flower arrangements. The bristle-like projections on the leaves have been used to create 'flies' for fishing, because they twist and untwist when on a moist surface.

Height: 75–90 cm (2½–3 ft).

Spread: 45 cm (1½ ft).

Soil and situation: Light, moderately fertile, moisture-retentive but well-drained soil preferably in full sun.

Raising new plants: Sow seeds in spring, each year (see page 60).

Briza maxima

Great Quaking Grass (UK)
Pearl Grass (UK) **Puffed Wheat** (UK/USA)

Hardy annual grass with an upright habit. It develops narrow, pointed, bright green leaves and from late spring to mid-summer has long, heart-shaped spikelets borne loosely and pendulously.

Height: 38–50 cm (15–20 in), sometimes more.

Spread: 23 cm (9 in), sometimes more.

Soil and situation: Moderately fertile, well-drained but moisture-retentive soil in full sun.

Raising new plants: During spring, sow seeds shallowly where the plants are to grow. Thin the seedlings when large enough to handle (see page 60).

Briza media

Big Quaking Grass (USA) **Common Quaking Grass** (UK/USA)
Quaking Grass (UK/USA) **Rattling Grass** (UK/USA)
Trembling Grass (UK/USA)

Hardy, perennial, creeping grass with upright, slender stems and light green leaves. From spring to late summer it bears heart-shaped, purple-brown spikelets.

Height: 30–45 cm (12–18 in), sometimes more.

Spread: 15–20 cm (6–8 in), sometimes more.

Soil and situation: Moderately fertile, well-drained but moisture-retentive soil in full sun.

Raising new plants: Lift and divide congested plants in spring (see page 61).

Bromus briziformis

Brome (UK) **Rattlesnake Chess** (USA)

Hardy annual with downy leaves up to 15 cm (6 in) long. The leaves are sometimes dried and used in bouquets and flower arrangements.

Height: 50–60 cm (20–24 in).

Spread: 30–45 cm (12–18 in).

Soil and situation: Fertile, moisture-retentive but well-drained soil in full sun.

Raising new plants: Sow seeds in spring, each year (see page 60).

Calamagrostis x acutiflora 'Karl Foerster'

Feather Reedgrass (UK)

This hardy perennial and tufted grass has stiffly erect stems, arching green leaves and upright red-bronze flower clusters that later become buff.

Height: 1.8 m (6 ft).

Spread: 45–60 cm (18–24 in).

Soil and situation: Moderately fertile, moisture-retentive soil and slight shade. It grows quite well in moderately heavy soils, but they must be moisture-retentive and not dry out.

Raising new plants: Lift and divide congested plants in spring (see page 61).

Calamagrostis brachytricha

Korean Feather Reedgrass (UK)

Hardy, densely tufted perennial grass with stiffly erect stems.

Height: 1 m (3½ ft).

Spread: 45 cm (18 in).

Soil and situation: Moderately fertile, moisture-retentive soil and slight shade. It grows quite well in moderately heavy soils, but they must be moisture-retentive and not dry out.

Raising new plants: Lift and divide congested plants in spring (see page 61).

Carex elata 'Aurea'

Japanese Sedge Grass (UK/USA)
Variegated Tufted Sedge (UK/USA)

Also known as *Carex elata* 'Bowles' Golden', this beautiful sedge has bright golden-yellow leaves with thin green edges. It retains its beautiful colours throughout most of summer. The form 'Knightshayes' is another popular and highly attractive variegated plant, with yellow leaves.

Height: 30–35 cm (12–15 in).

Spread: 38–45 cm (15–18 in).

Soil and situation: Fertile, neutral or slightly acid, moisture-retentive but well-drained soil and full sun or partial shade.

Raising new plants: Lift and divide congested plants in spring (see page 61).

Carex oshimensis 'Evergold'

Variegated Japanese Sedge Grass (UK/USA)

Also known as *Carex morrowii* 'Evergold' and *Carex elata* 'Evergold', this beautiful sedge has an evergreen nature, rounded stance and stiff, arching leaves variegated green and yellow. It is ideal for planting in a large pot or small tub on a patio.

Height: 30–35 cm (12–15 in).

Spread: 38–45 cm (15–18 in).

Soil and situation: Fertile, neutral or slightly acid, moisture-retentive but well-drained soil and full sun or partial shade.

Raising new plants: Lift and divide congested plants in spring (see page 61).

Carex phyllocephala 'Sparkler'

Also known as *Carex phyllocephala* 'Fuiri Tenjiku-suge', this evergreen sedge has lime green to dark green leaves with white edges. Sometimes there are also white stripes or streaks on the leaves.

Height: 30–45 cm (12–18 in).

Spread: 38–45 cm (15–18 in).

Soil and situation: Fertile, neutral or slightly acid, moisture-retentive but well-drained soil and full sun or partial shade.

Raising new plants: Lift and divide congested plants in spring (see page 61).

Carex testacea

Hardy, clump-forming sedge from New Zealand, densely but loosely tufted and packed with narrow, pale olive leaves that appear orange-tinted when in full sun. As well as being ideal for path edges and borders, it can be planted in containers on patios. The form 'Old Gold' has bright, bronze-orange leaves.

Height: 45–60 cm (18–24 in).

Spread: 45–60 cm (18–24 in), sometimes slightly more.

Soil and situation: Fertile, neutral or slightly acid, moisture-retentive but well-drained soil and full sun.

Raising new plants: Lift and divide congested plants in spring (see page 61).

Coix lacryma-jobi

Christ's Tears (UK) **Job's Tears** (UK/USA)

Distinctive half-hardy annual with a tufted habit and broad, lance-shaped, pale to mid-green leaves. The stems arch and from mid-summer to early autumn bear edible seeds in tear-like clusters.

Height: 45–60 cm (18–24 in).

Spread: 20–23 cm (8–9 in).

Soil and situation: Fertile, moisture-retentive but well-drained soil in full sun.

Raising new plants: During late winter and early spring, sow seeds shallowly in pots placed in a greenhouse with a temperature of 13–16°C (55–61°F). After germination, transfer the seedlings to wider spacings in seed-trays, and as soon as all risk of frost has passed plant them into a garden. Alternatively, sow seeds outdoors in mid-spring where they are to grow.

Cortaderia selloana

Pampas Grass (UK/USA)

Also known as *Cortaderia argentea*, this hardy, perennial, dominant evergreen grass with slender, arching, rough-edged, mid- to dark green leaves develops tall stems, which bear 38–45 cm (15–18 in) long silvery plumes at their tops during late summer and early autumn. There are many forms, including 'Pumila' (compact and small at 1.5–1.8 m/5–6 ft) high) and 'Sunningdale Silver' (more dominant and with large, white plumes). Two forms with variegated leaves include 'Albolineata' (also known as 'Silver Stripe') and 'Aureolineata' (also known as 'Gold Band').

Height: 1.8–2.4 m (6–8 ft), some are smaller.

Spread: 1.5–1.8 m (5–6 ft), some are smaller.

Soil and situation: Well-drained, fertile soil and full sun.

Raising new plants: Lift and divide congested plants in spring.

Deschampsia cespitosa 'Golden Dew'

Golden Tufted Hair Grass (USA)

Also known as *Deschampsia cespitosa* 'Goldtau', this hardy perennial grass forms compact tufts of deep rich green leaves and fountains of tall, green stems in early summer. Later they mellow to a haze of golden-brown. There are several other superb forms, including *Deschampsia cespitosa* 'Gold Veil' (also known as *Deschampsia cespitosa* 'Goldschleier') with tufts of dark green, overlapping leaves from which emerge plumes of green stems and flowers that later assume a warm golden-yellow glow.

Height: 75 cm (2½ ft).

Spread: 45–50 cm (18–20 in).

Soil and situation: Moderately fertile, moisture-retentive but well-drained soil in semi-shade.

Raising new plants: Lift and divide congested plants in spring.

Festuca glauca

Blue Fescue (UK) **Grey Fescue** (UK/USA)

Hardy perennial grass with a tufted nature and narrow, bristle-like, beautiful blue-grey leaves. During early and mid-summer it bears purple spikelets on stems about 30 cm (1 ft) long. There are several varieties, some dwarf but most with blue, blue-green or silvery-blue leaves.

Height: 15–23 cm (6–9 in).

Spread: 15–20 cm (6–8 in).

Soil and situation: Light, well-drained soil and full sun. Can be planted in a container.

Raising new plants: Lift and divide congested plants in early spring (see page 61).

Glycera maxima variegata

Variegated Manna Grass (UK/USA)
Variegated Reed Sweetgrass (UK)

Also known as *Glyceria spectabilis* 'Variegata' and *Glyceria aquatica variegata*, this hardy, herbaceous grass is invasive. The tall, rather relaxed and arching leaves have pinkish-white stripes in spring, but as the season progresses the pink fades. It is best planted in a container that prevents its spread.

Height: 75–90 cm (2½–3 ft).

Spread: 75–90 cm (2½–3 ft).

Soil and situation: Moisture-retentive soil in a bog garden, or as a marginal plant at the edge of a pond and in water up to 15 cm (6 in) deep. It grows best when in full sun.

Raising new plants: Lift and divide congested plants in spring (see page 61).

Hakonechloa macra 'Alboaurea'

Hardy perennial grass with a cascading habit. The long and narrow leaves are striped gold and off-white, with little green. It is ideal for planting in a border, and especially at the edge of a raised bed, as well as in a container. There are several other superb forms of this stunningly attractive plant, including 'Aureola' with yellow leaves striped green, and assuming pink-red shades in autumn.

Height: 30–38 cm (12–15 in).

Spread: 38–45 cm (15–18 in).

Soil and situation: Moderately fertile, well-drained but moisture-retentive soil and light shade.

Raising new plants: Lift and divide congested plants in spring (see page 61).

Holcus mollis 'Albovariegatus'

Variegated Creeping Soft Grass (UK/USA)

Also known as *Holcus mollis* 'Variegatus', this hardy perennial grass – a less invasive form of the species – displays leaves striped alternately silver and grey green.

Height: 30–45 cm (12–18 in).

Spread: 30–38 cm (12–15 in).

Soil and situation: Neutral or slightly acid, moisture-retentive but well-drained soil in full sun.

Raising new plants: Lift and divide congested plants in spring (see page 61); this variegated form cannot be raised from seeds.

Hordeum jubatum

Fox-tail Barley (UK/USA) **Squirrel-tail Barley** (UK/USA)
Squirrel-tail Grass (UK/USA)

Hardy annual – occasionally perennial and with a tufted habit in mild climates – with an upright form and arching leaves.

Height: 45–60 cm (18–24 in).

Spread: 30–45 cm (12–18 in).

Soil and situation: Moderately fertile, light, moisture-retentive but well-drained soil and full sun.

Raising new plants: Sow seeds in spring, each year (see page 60). However, plants often persist from one year to another.

Miscanthus sacchariflorus

Amur Silver Grass (USA) **Hardy Sugar Cane** (UK/USA)
Silver Banner Grass (UK)

Hardy grass with creeping rhizomatous roots and tall stems bearing narrow, mid-green, arching leaves. The form 'Variegatus' has leaves with white stripes.

Height: 2.4–3 m (8–10 ft).

Spread: 90 cm (3 ft).

Soil and situation: Light, moisture-retentive soil and full sun.

Raising new plants: Lift and divided congested clumps in early or mid-spring (see page 61).

Miscanthus sinensis 'Variegatus'

Japanese Variegated Silver Grass (UK)
Variegated Eulalia (USA)

Hardy, rhizomatous-rooted and clump-forming perennial grass with initially upright and rigid leaves that later semi-cascade. The green leaves are attractively variegated creamy-white.

Height: 1.2–1.5 m (4–5 ft), sometimes more.

Spread: 45–60 cm (18–24 in), sometimes more.

Soil and situation: Light, moisture-retentive soil and full sun.

Raising new plants: Lift and divided congested clumps in early or mid-spring (see page 61).

OTHER FORMS OF
MISCANTHUS SINENSIS

- 'Goldfeder' (also known as 'Gold Feather'), sometimes known as Golden Variegated Miscanthus, produces graceful clumps of broad leaves striped and edged in golden-yellow. It grows 1.8–2.1 m (6–7 ft) high.

- 'Morning Light' produces dense, erect clumps of green, creamy-white edged leaves. It grows 1.2–1.5 m (4–5 ft) high.

- *purpurascens* (also known as *Miscanthus* 'Purpurascens') has a robust nature and foliage handsomely tinged purple. It grows 1.5 m (5 ft) high.

- 'Silver Feather' (also known as 'Silberfeder') develops green leaves and silvery plumes. It grows about 2.1 m (7 ft) high.

- 'Zebrinus' (Zebra Grass) has irregular yellow cross-banding on a green background. It grows about 1.5 m (5 ft) high.

Miscanthus sinensis 'Cabaret' is a particularly boldly variegated form

Molinia caerulea 'Variegata'

Variegated Moor Grass (UK)

Hardy perennial, slow-growing grass with a neat and compact habit. The dark green leaves are striped creamy-white.

Height: 45 cm (18 in)

Spread: 30–45 cm (12–18 in)

Soil and situation: Fertile, moisture-retentive but well-drained, neutral or slightly acid soil in light shade.

Raising new plants: Lift and divide congested plants in spring (see page 61).

Pennisetum alopecuroides

Chinese Pennisetum (UK/USA) **Fountain Grass** (UK)
Swamp Foxglove (UK)

Also known as *Pennisetum compressum*, this half-hardy perennial grass is long-lived, and has narrow, grey-green leaves. During early and mid-autumn, it produces feathery, tawny-yellow, 5–15 cm (2–6 in) long plumes of flowers. There are many attractive forms.

Height: 90 cm (3 ft).

Spread: 45–60 cm (18–24 in).

Soil and situation: Light, well-drained but moisture-retentive soil in full sun.

Raising new plants: Lift and divide congested plants in spring (see page 61).

Pennisetum setaceum

Feather Grass (UK/USA) **Tender Fountain Grass** (UK)

Also known as *Pennesetum rueppellii*, this half-hardy, tufted, perennial grass has rough-textured, narrow, mid-green leaves. From mid-summer to early autumn it produces feathery heads, up to 30 cm (1 ft) long, of cream-green, silky spikelets which are often tinged purple. There are several attractive forms, including 'Rubrum' with red leaves.

Height: 90 cm (3 ft).

Spread: 45–60 cm (18–24 in).

Soil and situation: Light, well-drained but moisture-retentive soil in full sun.

Raising new plants: Lift and divide congested plants in spring (see page 61).

Pennisetum villosum

Feather Grass (UK) **Feathertop** (USA)

Also known as *Pennisetum longistylum*, this half-hardy perennial grass is usually raised as a half-hardy annual. It develops slender, hairy stems and narrow, arching, mid-green leaves. During early and mid-summer it bears white, sometimes tawny-brown or purple flowers.

Height: 45–60 cm (18–24 in).

Spread: 25–30 cm (10–12 in).

Soil and situation: Light, well-drained but moisture-retentive soil in full sun.

Raising new plants: Sow seeds in early spring in pots in a greenhouse. Place in 15–17°C (59–63°F), and when large enough to handle transfer the seedlings to wider spacings in seed-trays. Plant into a garden when all risk of frost has passed.

Phalaris arundinacea var. picta

Gardeners' Garters (UK/USA) **Ribbon Grass** (USA)

Hardy, perennial, rhizomatous-rooted grass with a spreading, relaxed and informal nature. It develops narrow leaf-blades with cream and bright green longitudinal stripes. The lower leaves tend to arch, while the central ones are more upright.

Height: 60 cm (2 ft).

Spread: 45–60 cm (18–24 in).

Soil and situation: Well-drained, moderately fertile soil and full sun or light shade.

Raising new plants: Lift and divide congested plants in mid-autumn or mid-spring (see page 61).

Spartina pectinata 'Aureomarginata'

Freshwater Cord Grass (USA)
Prairie Cord Grass (UK/USA) **Slough Grass** (UK/USA)

Rhizomatous-rooted perennial grass with a robust and tufted nature. It develops a mass of initially upright, then arching, narrow, olive-green leaves with golden edges. Additionally, it has tall, green flower spikes with purple anthers.

Height: 90 cm–1.5 m (3–5 ft).

Spread: 1.2–1.5 m (4–5 ft).

Soil and situation: Moderately fertile, moisture-retentive soil and full sun.

Raising new plants: Lift and divide congested plants in spring (see page 61).

Stipa calamagrostis

Silver Spike Grass (UK/USA)

Perennial, clump-forming grass with a dense and compact but wind-blown appearance. It develops tufts of narrow, grey-green leaves and stems that bear the silvery buff-violet flower plumes, up to 30 cm (1 ft) long, from early summer to early autumn.

Height: 90 cm–1.2 m (3–4 ft).

Spread: 60–75 cm (2–2½ ft).

Soil and situation: Light, fertile, well-drained but moisture-retentive soil in full sun.

Raising new plants: Lift and divide congested plants in spring (see page 61).

Stipa gigantea

Giant Feather Grass (UK/USA)

Hardy, long-lived, nearly evergreen perennial grass with a grassy, clump-forming nature and thin, grey-green leaves, 60–90 cm (2–3 ft) long. It also develops 23–30 cm (9–12 in) long, silvery purple-tinged flower plumes on stiff, upright stems during early and mid-summer.

Height: 90 cm–1.2 m (3–4 ft).

Spread: 60–75 cm (2–2½ ft).

Soil and situation: Light, fertile, moisture-retentive soil in full sun.

Raising new plants: Lift and divide congested plants in spring (see page 61).

Stipa tenuissima

This hardy perennial grass is one of the most graceful and relaxed grasses, forming bright green clumps with fluffy plumes.

Height: 60–75 cm (2–2½ ft).

Spread: 60–75 cm (2–2½ ft).

Soil and situation: Light, fertile, well-drained but moisture-retentive soil in full sun.

Raising new plants: Lift and divide congested plants in spring (see page 61).

Zea mays

Corn (USA) **Corn-on-the-cob** (UK) **Field Corn** (USA) **Indian Corn** (UK) **Maize** (USA) **Pod Corn** (USA) **Sweet Corn** (UK/USA) **Volunteer Corn** (USA)

Half-hardy annual grass widely grown for the upright, cob-like clusters of edible seeds. However, it is the ornamental forms that are grown for decorating borders, perhaps in summer bedding schemes or to fill gaps in herbaceous borders.

Ornamental varieties include 'Quadricolor', which has leaves variegated white, pink and pale yellow. It is a robust variety and is also known as 'Gigantea Quadricolor'. 'Japonica' has green leaves striped in cream or white, while 'Harlequin Mixed' has leaves striped in many colours.

Height: 1.2–1.5 m (4–5 ft).

Spread: 23–30 cm (9–12 in).

Soil and situation: Fertile, light, moisture-retentive but well-drained soil and a wind-sheltered, sunny position.

Raising new plants: Raise either as half-hardy annuals sown in gentle warmth in mid-spring and later hardened off before planting outdoors, or as hardy annuals where seeds are sown in late spring where plants are to grow (see page 60).

FURTHER GRASSES AND SEDGES TO CONSIDER

• *Anemanthele lessoniana* Hardy perennial grass, usually raised from seed. It develops beautiful arching leaves, with strands of ruby-red shining through the lime-green background. It is ideal in a border as well as in a container. Height: 90 cm (3 ft).

• *Anthoxanthmum gracile* Known as the Annual Vernal Grass, it is a hardy annual, with loose tussocks of arching leaves. It grows to 20–30 cm (8–12 in) in height.

• *Carex flagillifera* Hardy perennial sedge, forming a dome of pale bronze to tawny-green leaves. It is ideal for planting in containers or in a border. Height: 45–60 cm (18–24 in).

• *Carex pilulifera* **'Tinney's Princess'** Hardy, dwarf, tufted sedge, known as the Pill Sedge, with green leaves that have creamy-yellow central stripes. Height: 25–30 cm (10–12 in).

• *Eleusine coracana* Widely known as African Millet, Coracan, Finger Millet and Kurakkan, this half-hardy annual has a tufted habit, producing many green, claw-like flowers throughout summer. It is ideal as a cut flower and for growing in a border. Height: 45–60 cm (18–24 in).

• *Lagurus ovatus* Known as Hare's Tail on account of its soft, silky, fur-like flowerheads, it is raised as a half-hardy annual. Height: 45 cm (18 in).

• *Melica altissima* **'Atropurpurea'** Known as the Siberian Melic, this hardy perennial grass produces deep mauve spikelets. It is ideal for planting towards the back of a border where it can contrast with other plants. It is also superb for including in dried-flower arrangements. Height: 1.2 m (4 ft).

• *Panicum virgatum* Known as Switch Grass, this clump-forming hardy perennial grass has upright, steely-blue leaves. In autumn, the colour changes to soft yellow. Height: 90 cm (3 ft).

• *Sporobolus pulchellus* Known as the Dropseed and Rush Grass, this hardy annual may become a perennial when grown in a warm position. Height: 30–35 cm (12–14 in).

• *Stipa pennata* Known as the European Feather Grass and Feather Grass, it is perennial, and it has narrow, mid-green leaves and silvery-buff, feathery, loose heads of flowers. Height: 60–75 cm (2–2½ ft).

Buying, looking after and increasing palms

Are palms easy to grow?

Once established, palms are easily grown. Those that are grown indoors or in conservatories need a winter temperature of 10–16°C (50–61°F), together with light shade, especially in summer. Outdoor palms growing in temperate climates are only successful if you select relatively hardy ones (see pages 74–75). A few indoor palms can be put outside in summer, but if they are left there invariably the winter weather soon kills them.

The distinctive fan-shaped leaves of Chamaerops humilis *(Dwarf Fan Palm).*

BUYING PALMS

Here are a few clues to buying a palm, whether for the home or garden:
- Buy from a reputable source to ensure that the palm has not been dug up in the wild and that rare species have not been put at risk.
- Look under and above leaves for signs of pests and diseases (see opposite page).
- Check that the container is not too small; this could constrict the roots.
- The compost should be slightly moist, but not saturated.
- Check that the plant is labelled.

GETTING THE SOIL RIGHT

Palms in the wild grow in a wide range of soils, but most of them need fertile, well-drained but moisture-retentive soil that is slightly acid (pH 6.0 to 6.5). When growing palms in containers indoors or in conservatories, choose loam-based potting compost. First place pieces of broken clay pots in the base of the container to enable excess water to escape.

PLANTING A PALM OUTDOORS

Late spring and early summer are the best times to plant an outdoor palm.
- Prepare the area several months before planting; remove the roots of perennial weeds and mix in bulky organic materials such as well-decomposed farmyard manure or garden compost.
- The day before planting, water the compost in the container. Also water the planting area; allow the surface soil to dry slightly before planting.
- Where the soil is well drained, plant the palm in the flat soil (see right). Dig out the hole and form and firm a slight mound in the base. Place the palm's soil ball on the mound, so that its surface is fractionally below the surrounding soil. Draw soil around the soil ball and firm it.
- Where the area is predominantly clay and badly drained, mound the soil to form a raised area (see right). Dig out the hole and plant in the same way as for a flat area.

On well-drained soil

Check that the top of the soil ball is fractionally below surface level

On badly drained soil

Create a large, wide, raised mound of soil and plant the palm in it

AFTER PLANTING ...
- Thoroughly water the soil.
- Spread a 7.5 cm (3 in) thick layer of well-decayed farmyard manure or well-decomposed garden compost over the soil. This helps to conserve moisture in the soil, and provides food for the palm.

LOOKING AFTER OUTDOOR PALMS

Feeding Palms demand plenty of food and respond to regular applications of fertilizers. In spring, before applying a mulch, dust the soil with a high-nitrogen fertilizer. About 2–3 months later, and in the latter part of summer, dust the soil with a balanced fertilizer. However, do not feed palms late in their growing season.

Watering Although many palms live in relatively dry regions, they all benefit from moist soil. The roots of palms spread widely and laterally, and therefore it is essential to thoroughly soak a wide area. This is best undertaken during evenings or early mornings, when the chance of water immediately evaporating is low.

Mulching Palms are shallow-rooting plants, and a yearly mulch in late spring, after you have removed weeds and watered the soil, helps to feed plants, and keeps the soil cool and moist.

Pruning Palms need little pruning, other than the removal in spring of dead fronds and the remains of clusters of fruits. Old fronds are sometimes left around some palms to create an unusual and attractive feature, but eventually they encourage vermin and are potential fire hazards. Take care not to damage the palm's growing point, as it will die.

Dealing with suckers Misplaced suckers are always best removed. You can remove large suckers by digging down and severing them with a sharp knife, and restrain those that appear in a lawn by regularly mowing over them. Suckering palms, when grown as single-trunked ornamental palms, can be made more attractive by removing any suckers growing from their base.

INCREASING PALMS

- **Seeds:** Fresh seed and high temperatures of up to 35°C (95°F) – depending on the species – are essential. Later, high humidity is needed to prevent the seedlings shrivelling and to ensure rapid growth. Sow seed in compost in seed-trays, ensuring that individual seeds do not touch. Place the seed-tray in a propagation frame with bottom heat and keep the compost moist. After germination, reduce the temperature slightly and, later, transfer the seedlings to small but deep, individual pots. Until established, keep them in light shade and gentle warmth.

- **Offsets:** This is an excellent way for home gardeners to produce a few new plants and is best undertaken in late spring or early summer. Use a spade or trowel to draw soil from around the base of an offset. Use a sharp knife to remove the offset from the parent; sometimes an offset has roots, and these have a better chance of survival than offsets that do not. If you notice a lack of roots before you have entirely removed the offset, partially sever the offset's base and repack soil around it. Later, when roots have formed, remove it. Transfer the rooted offsets to individual pots and keep them watered and lightly shaded until they are well established.

Increasing palms by offsets is an easy way to propagate sucker-forming species.

GERMINATING SEEDS IN POLYTHENE BAGS

As a space-saving way to germinate palm seeds, mix them with moist peat and place in a strong, clear, polythene bag. Seal the bag and place it in a warm, shaded greenhouse, perhaps under the staging. Avoid positions in direct sun as this overheats the compost. When you can see roots and leaves, transfer them into individual pots.

After mixing the seeds with moist peat, place the bag in shade in a greenhouse.

TROUBLESHOOTING WITH PALMS

Apart from damage from pests, such as scale insects, red spider mites and mealy bugs (see right), leaves can become unsightly through cultural reasons.

- **Excessively wet compost:** Encourages leaf spot disease (caused by a bacteria and producing dark brown spots on the leaves). Cut off infected leaves and spray with a fungicide.
- **Dry compost:** Leaves assume yellow shades, especially during summer. Thoroughly moisten the compost.
- **Dry air:** Leaves assume a dull colour and tips become brown and dry. Regularly mist spray plants, especially during hot weather. Check that the compost is moist, but not waterlogged.

Three pests to watch out for:
- **Scale insects:** When young and at the 'crawler' stage, scale insects are relatively easy to eradicate by wiping them off with a cotton bud dipped in methylated spirits. You can also use oil-based sprays. Later, when the insects are protected by a scale-like cover, eradication is difficult and repeated sprays are necessary at two-week intervals with a systemic insecticide.
- **Red spider mites:** These near-microscopic, spider-like, eight-legged creatures cluster on the undersides of leaves, sucking sap and causing yellowing and mottling. Mist-spraying plants with clean water deters them. Also use an acaricide.
- **Mealy bugs:** These resemble small, white, wax-covered woodlice. They cluster under leaves and around junctions of stems and leaves, sucking sap and causing weakness in the palm. Dry compost intensifies the problem. Eradicate small infestations on indoor palms by wiping them with methylated-spirits. Alternatively, use a systemic insecticide.

Palms for temperate climates

There are only a few palms that can be grown outdoors in temperate regions, and even then they need a warm and wind-protected position. Some palms grown as houseplants in temperate climates are sufficiently hardy to be put outdoors during summer in a sheltered position. However, palms are ideal for creating stately and permanent displays in conservatories, and in earlier times the foyers of grand hotels were often peppered with them.

Trachycarpus fortunei *(Windmill Palm) will grow outdoors in mild temperate regions, but needs wind protection.*

Chamaerops humilis

Dwarf Fan Palm (UK) **European Fan Palm** (USA) **Fan Palm** (USA) **Mediterranean Fan Palm** (UK/USA)

Slightly less hardy than *Trachycarpus fortunei* (Chusan Palm), this shrubby, evergreen, European palm usually forms a dense cluster of growths close to the ground, but it can also create a small tree. The fan-shaped leaves, formed of 12–15 greyish-green segments, are borne on slender, spiny leaf-stalks. The trunk becomes clothed in stiff, dark fibres.

Height: Up to 2.4 m (8 ft).

Spread: 1.2–1.8 m (4–6 ft).

Soil and situation: Well-drained but moisture-retentive soil that is neither strongly acid nor alkaline, and full sun or light shade. It is only hardy enough to be grown outdoors in warmer areas in temperate climates, and only then when it is sheltered from cold winds.

Raising new plants: In the same way as for *Trachycarpus fortunei* (see opposite).

Phoenix canariensis *(Canary Island Date Palm) is used in bedding displays in warm regions to create a Mediterranean aura.*

PLANT USES

Chamaerops humilis is native to southern Europe, where its young leaf buds were once eaten locally as a vegetable; the fibres also provided cordage. Indeed, about 100 years ago this palm was widely grown for its fibre, which was used as a substitute for horsehair in upholstery. The dried leaves have also been used for making baskets.

Trachycarpus fortunei

Chinese Windmill Palm (USA) **Chusan Palm** (UK)
Hemp Palm (USA) **Windmill Palm** (UK/USA)

Also known as *Trachycarpus excelsa* and *Chamaerops excelsa*, this slow-growing, evergreen palm develops large fans, often 90 cm (3 ft) wide and formed of narrow, folded segments borne on stalks up to 90 cm (3 ft) long. The trunk is clothed in black, coarse, hairy fibres.

There are several other species, including *Trachycarpus wagnerianus*, which is smaller and has leaves formed of small, stiff segments. *Trachycarpus martianus* is not as hardy as *Trachycarpus excelsa* and develops leaves divided to about halfway. The segments droop towards their tips. *Trachycarpus takil* bears more resemblance to *Trachycarpus fortunei* than to *Trachycarpus martianus* and has less-divided leaves.

Height: 3–3.6 m (10–12 ft) or more.

Spread: 1.8–3 m (6–10 ft).

Soil and situation: Well-drained but moisture-retentive soil, neither strongly acid nor alkaline, and full sun or light shade. It is the only palm that is hardy enough to be grown outdoors in temperate climates, but a position sheltered from cold winds is essential. It is ideal for introducing a Mediterranean atmosphere to patios, especially those with a southerly aspect. Alternatively, plant it as a specimen palm on the side of a sunny patio.

Raising new plants: In late spring, cut off large suckers from around the plant's base and pot up into loam-based compost. Place in a greenhouse where 10–13°C (50–55°F) can be maintained. When rooted, reduce the temperature and plant into a nursery bed.

PLANT USES

In China, the fibres that cover the trunk of Trachycarpus fortunei *have been used to make cordage and brushes, and the leaves have been employed in the making of rough coats and hats.*

PALMS FOR MEDITERRANEAN CLIMATES

Several palms are popular in Mediterranean countries, where they are grown either as ornamental features or for their commercial value. Apart from *Trachycarpus fortunei* and *Chamaerops humilis*, other palms include:

- *Phoenix canariensis* The popular Canary Island Date Palm is widely grown in warm temperate and subtropical regions as an avenue palm. It develops shiny, mid-green leaflets on leaves that are 3–6 m (10–20 ft) long and have a distinctive drooping habit. In the wild, it grows 15–21 m (50–70 ft) high, but less in cultivation.

- *Phoenix dactylifera* Known as the Date Palm, it has greyish-green leaflets with a light and near-imperceptible bluish blush. In tropical and subtropical regions, it is grown as an avenue tree, as well as in clusters where it creates distinctive features. In the wild, it grows to 24–30 m (80–100 ft) high, but only 15–18 m (50–60 ft) in cultivation.

- *Washingtonia filifera* This is the popular Californian Fan Palm, with yellow-green to greyish-green, narrow and tapering segments forming fan-shaped leaves, 1.8–2.4 m (6–8 ft) wide and borne on 1.8 m (6 ft) long leaf-stalks. It creates a distinctive ornamental feature, as well as being used as a street tree. In the wild, it grows to 18 m (60 ft) high, but less in cultivation. A related species, *Washingtonia robusta* (Washington Palm, Mexican Fan Palm) grows taller and is often used in warm climates as an avenue palm.

A–Z of indoor palms

Awide range of palms can be grown indoors and in conservatories in temperate climates. They include varieties with feather-like foliage and ones with leaves that form attractive and characteristic fans. Other palms have cane-like stems or leaves with ends that resemble fish tails. The palm-like cycad *Cycas revoluta* (Sago Palm) is another possibility. Both palms and cycads introduce a dignified stateliness to homes and conservatories.

INDOOR PALMS FOR TEMPERATE CLIMATES

Palms grown indoors and in conservatories can be arranged into four groups – 'Cane Palms', 'Feather Palms', 'Fan Palms' and 'Fishtail' types.

Please note: The heights and spreads given are for palms grown indoors or in conservatories, not for those grown outdoors in warm climates.

Cane Palms

• *Chamaedorea erumpens*
Characteristically known as the Bamboo Palm, it forms clusters of cane-like stems that bear fronds with deep green leaflets.
Height: 1.5–3 m (5–10 ft). Spread: 75 cm–1.2 m (2½–4 ft).

• *Chamaedorea seifrizii*
Known as the Reed Palm, it has a similar nature to *Chamaedorea erumpens*, but has up to 18 long and narrow, deep green leaflets on each frond.
Height: 1.5–3 m (5–10 ft). Spread: 75 cm–1.5 m (2½–5 ft).

• *Chrysalidocarpus lutescens*
Also known as *Areca lutescens* and commonly as Areca Palm, Butterfly Palm, Cane Palm, Golden Cane Palm or Yellow Palm, it has a dominant nature. Sometimes it is sold as *Dypsis lutescens*. It develops cane-like stems and feather-like clusters of yellowish-green leaflets.
Height: 1.5–3 m (5–10 ft).
Spread: 90 cm–1.5 m (3–5 ft).

Chrysalidocarpus lutescens

Feather Palms

• *Chamaedorea elegans*
Also called *Neanthe bella*, it is commonly known as the Good-luck Palm and Parlour Palm. It produces mid- to dark green, fairly wide leaflets on arching stems.
Height: 45 cm–1.2 m (1½–4 ft).
Spread: 45–75 cm (1½–2½ ft).

Chamaedorea elegans

• *Howea belmoreana*
Also called *Howeia belmoreana* and *Kentia belmoreana*, it is commonly known as Belmore Sentry Palm, Curly Palm and Sentry Palm. It develops large, graceful, arching fronds up to 30 cm (1 ft) wide.
Height: 1.8–3 m (6–10 ft).
Spread: 1.5–2.4 m (5–8 ft).

Howea belmoreana

• *Howea forsteriana*
Also known as *Howeia forsteriana* and *Kentia forsteriana,* and popularly as Kentia Palm, Paradise Palm, Sentry Palm, Thatch Leaf Palm and Thatch Palm, it forms a dominant feature with its large, wide, deep green leaflets. The stems are less arching than those of *Howea belmoreana*.
Height: 1.8–3 m (6–10 ft). Spread: 1.5–2.4 m (5–8 ft).

• *Lytocaryum weddellianum*
Popularly known as Dwarf Coconut Palm and Weddel Palm, it is also called *Microcoelum weddellianum, Syagrus weddelliana* and *Cocos weddelliana*. It is diminutive and often claimed to be the prettiest palm, with slightly arching fronds bearing narrow, mid- to dark green leaflets. Even after 15 or so years, it reaches only 1.5–1.8 m (5–6 ft) high.
Height: 23–38 cm (9–15 in) during its early years.
Spread: 23–30 cm (9–12 in) during its early years.

• *Phoenix canariensis*
Distinctive palm known as the Canary Date Palm, Canary Island Date Palm and Canary Palm. It develops feather-like fronds with narrow leaflets on arching stems.
Height: 1.2–1.8 m (4–6 ft). Spread: 90 cm–1.5 m (3–5 ft).

• *Phoenix roebelenii*
Popularly known as the Miniature Date Palm, Pygmy Date Palm and Roebelin Palm, it is almost stemless, with feather-type fronds formed of dark green leaves with many narrow leaflets.
Height: 90 cm–1.2 m (3–4 ft). Spread: 60–90 cm (2–3 ft).

INDOOR PALMS FOR TEMPERATE CLIMATES (CONTINUED)

Fan Palms

- *Chamaerops humilis*
Known as the Dwarf Fan Palm, European Fan Palm, Fan Palm and Mediterranean Fan Palm, it can be grown outdoors in warm temperate climates, but also does well indoors. See page 74 for a description.
Height: 90 cm–1.5 m (3–5 ft).
Spread: 90 cm–1.5 m (3–5 ft).

- *Livistonia chinensis*
Known as the Chinese Fan Palm, Chinese Fountain Palm and Fan Palm, it is slow-growing when indoors, and produces large, bright green, segmented fans with drooping tips.
Height: 1.2–3 m (4–10 ft).
Spread: 60 cm–1 m (2–3½ ft).

Livistonia chinensis

- *Rhapsis excelsa*
Popularly known as the Bamboo Palm, Broad-leaved Lady Palm, Fern Rhapsis, Ground Rattan, Little Lady Palm and Miniature Fan Palm, it is clump-forming. It develops bamboo-like stems and mid- to dark green, finger-like leaves that radiate from their tops like a fan. Each of the leaves is about 20 cm (8 in) long.
Height: 90 cm–1.5 m (4–5 ft). Spread: 75–90 cm (2½–3 ft).

Rhapsis excelsa

Fishtail Palms

- *Caryota mitis*
Known as the Burmese Fishtail Palm, Clustered Fishtail Palm, Fishtail Palm and Tufted Fishtail Palm, it develops ragged-ended, wedge-shaped, thick, dark green leaflets that eventually are 15 cm (6 in) long and 10 cm (4 in) wide. They are borne on arching stems.
Height: 1.5–2.4 m (5–8 ft). Spread: 60 cm–1 m (2–3½ ft).

Caryota mitis

- *Caryota urens*
This is the Fishtail Palm, Jaggery Palm, Kittul Palm, Solitary Fishtail Palm, Toddy Palm and Wine Palm; it develops bright green, shiny, wedge-shaped and slightly triangular leaflets.
Height: 1.8–2.4 m (6–8 ft). Spread: 60 cm–1 m (2–3½ ft).

CYCAS REVOLUTA

Known as the Sago Palm, Japanese Sago Palm and Japanese Fern palm, it is a cycad rather than a palm: it is frequently seen indoors, where its slow growth makes it a long-term resident. In Asia, its trunk has been a minor source of sago (a powdery starch used as a food thickener and textile stiffener), while the large, red seeds are eaten either raw or cooked.

USING PALMS INDOORS

Table-top arrangements including small palms create exciting displays.

A tall palm is an ideal companion for houseplants in a floor display.

Use a spotlight to illuminate a tall palm and create interesting wall shadows.

Glossary

Adventitious Occurring in an unusual position and often used to refer to roots and buds.

Annual A plant that grows from seed, flowers and dies within the same year.

Argenteus Silver-coloured.

Blind A shoot or plant without a growing point.

Clone A group of cultivated plants produced vegetatively from one original seedling or stock.

Container gardening Growing plants in containers, such as hanging-baskets, wall-baskets, windowboxes, tubs and pots.

Container-grown plant A plant that is sold growing and established in a container, ready for planting.

Culm A jointed stem – usually applied to bamboo canes.

Cultivar A cultivated variety.

Cycad An evergreen plant with a thick stem and crown of fernlike leaves that is similar in appearance to a palm.

Deciduous A plant that loses its leaves at the beginning of its dormant season – usually in autumn or early winter – and produces a fresh array of leaves in spring.

Division A vegetative method of propagation that involves splitting up a plant.

Evergreen A plant that continuously sheds and grows further leaves throughout the year, and therefore appears to be 'ever green'.

Genus A group of plants with similar botanical characteristics. Some genera contain many species, others just one.

Glabrous Smooth, not having hairs.

Glaucous Dull bluish-green, usually with a matt surface.

Ground cover A low-growing plant that forms a mat of foliage.

Half-hardy annual An annual that is raised in gentle warmth in spring, then acclimatized to outdoor temperatures before being planted into gardens and containers when all risk of frost has passed.

Hardy A plant that survives outdoors throughout the year and without any protection.

Hardy annual An annual that can be sown outdoors.

Herbaceous border A border planted with herbaceous plants. These create fresh growth each spring that dies down at the onset of winter.

Hybrid The progeny from parents of different species or genera.

Inflorescence The flowering part of a plant.

Internode The space between nodes on a stem.

Lanceolate Having the shape of a lance; used to describe the shape of a leaf.

Microclimate The climate within a small area, perhaps where it is protected from cold winds and where the warmth of the sun is not dissipated.

Mixed border A border formed of a mixture of plants and especially shrubs and herbaceous perennials.

Mulch A surface dressing or bulky organic material, such as well-decomposed manure or garden compost. It helps to conserve moisture in the soil, as well as keeping it cool. It also provides food for the roots.

Nana Small and dwarf.

Node The point on a stem – often swollen – where a leaf is joined on.

Relative humidity The ratio of water vapour in the air relative to the temperature.

Rhizome An underground or partly buried horizontal stem. They can be slender or fleshy.

Rootstock The part of a plant normally below the soil's surface.

Species A group of plants that breed together and have the same characteristics.

Synonym A previous botanical name for a plant. However, it frequently happens that a plant is better known and sold under the earlier name.

Type The true species, not a form.

Variegation Having two or more colours or shades or colour.

Windbreak A shrub, tree, conifer or bamboo used to reduce the speed of the wind and to create shelter for cultivated plants.

Index

Acknowledgments

AG&G Books would like to thank Stephen Evans of **Golden Days Garden Centre**, Back Lane, Appley Bridge, Standish, Wigan, WN6 8RS, Tel. 01257 423355, goldendaysgardencentre@btconnect.com and Manchester Road, Cheadle, Cheshire, SK8 2NZ, Tel. 0161 4283098, goldendays@btconnect.com, www.goldendaysgardencentre.com and Paul Whittaker of **PW Plants**, Sunnyside, Heath Road, Kenninghall, Norfolk, NR16 2DS, Tel: 01953 888212, www.hardybamboo.com/visit for supplying the majority of photographs in this book. Other photographs: AG&G Books and Garden Matters (pages 62BL, 63TL, 63BR, 64BL, 66TR, 67BR and 71R).